D1534833

VIRTUOSO PUBLICATIONS
206 S.E. 46th Lane
CAPE CORAL, FLORIDA 33904

Printed 1981 in the U.S.A.
Reprint of the 1904 edition
ISBN Number 0-918624-02-9
Virtuoso Publications
Harold Chaitman, Publisher
206 S.E. 46th Lane
Cape Coral, Florida 33904

PREFACE

THE casual observations which led to the interesting research which forms the subject of this Treatise came as a " bolt from the blue."

Experts who have had constant opportunities for studying the varnish on old Italian instruments have, without exception, accepted the theory that it is an oil-varnish coloured to suit individual taste, although in no single case have their own descriptions of its appearance been found to support this conclusion; various reasons and excuses have been suggested why modern violin-makers have been unable to reproduce it.

No scientist or chemist appears to have given much attention to the subject, for the simple reason that no means have been available for a complete investigation. There are, no doubt, many accomplished chemists who find recreation in the study of music, but it is not to be expected that one of these would sacrifice a favourite and valuable old instrument for the sake of obtaining a few grammes of varnish on the chance of being able to obtain from it some satisfactory information as to its composition; especially as he could have no reason to suspect the veracity of the dogma that it was a mere concoction.

Direct investigation of the causes of the colour effects of sunrise, sunset, of the rainbow, &c. was equally impossible; these natural and familiar phenomena were, for a long time, interpreted in accordance with the evidence of the senses, until scientific discovery of the composition, refraction and polarization of light afforded explanations which satisfied all the conditions.

It is not surprising that the old varnish, which could be judged only from its appearance, its softness, elasticity, and its solubility in alcohol, should have been interpreted in a similar simple fashion.

The theory offered to explain its composition was accepted, for want of a better one; it has now been tested for at least half-a-century, varnishes have been constantly produced in accordance with it; they have not been found to satisfy all the conditions: in fact, do they satisfy one of them ? The modern varnishes are not like the old ones in body (pâte), in transparency, in colour, in refraction, the instruments which they clothe are not comparable with the old ones in tone.

If from the apologists for the old theory information is sought as to the actual constituents of the varnish, the result is equally unsatisfactory: a gum for the basis is vaguely suggested, but eludes definition; colouring matters, soluble in alcohol, are mentioned, but the difficulty is overlooked that alcohol, of sufficient strength for their solution and admixture, was certainly not available in the sixteenth century; the further suggestion, that red colouring matters, soluble in oil of turpentine, existed then, but have ceased to exist now, will not pass: for it is easy to show that such red colouring matter is a scientific impossibility.

From every point of view, therefore, the dogma which has been so long and so persistently promulgated is found to be unsatisfactory.

The explanation of the mystery which is now offered is that the old violin-makers used as the constituents of their varnishes the natural products of trees (conifers) and plants (flax) growing in their immediate vicinity, abundant and easily procured; that they were simple varnishes composed of resin and turpentine, or of these two substances and linseed-oil; that the various apparent colours were due to optical effects naturally arising from variations in the details of the preparation of the varnishes; that the differences in their physical qualities arose from the same causes.

On careful examination it will certainly be found that this new theory satisfies every one of the required conditions and fully explains all the observed facts.

All that I ask from my readers is an impartial judgment on the evidence; magna est veritas, et prævalebit !

It is conceived that my own opinion is now the less likely to be warped from the consideration that, although my researches originated in the varnish question, this has long since become subsidiary to other and more absorbing problems which have arisen, which have completely over-shadowed the original one. From a scientific point of view (physiological and chemical), the constitution of the terpenes, whence they come and whither they go, are questions which will be fascinating long after the minor problem, of the constitution of the old varnishes and their influence on tone, has been set at rest.

G. F.

Berwick-on-Tweed, 1904.

CONTENTS

—◆—

CHAPTER 3

The tone of violins

CHAPTER 4

On the manufacture of oil-varnish

CHAPTER 5

Oil-varnish from turpentine derivatives and its application

CHAPTER 6

CHAPTER 7

CONCLUSION

THE
Varnishes of the Italian Violin-makers

CHAPTER 1

INTRODUCTION

THE gradual evolution of Violins (this term is used generically to include instruments of all sizes) from the ancient viols, traced after diligent research, has been well described by several writers. By means of workmen, unlearned but intelligent and skilful, this evolution appears to have been, in the main, a natural process from its origin in Brescia in the fifteenth to its perfection in Cremona in the beginning of the eighteenth century.

The introduction of the sound-post, however, an innovation of the utmost importance, appears to stand apart from this natural evolution of form. M. Vidal refers this invention to the " Trompetta marina " (illustrations of this curious instrument are given by him and by Naumann). In this instrument one foot of the bridge rests firmly upon the table (sounding-board), while the other foot approaches it so closely as to facilitate the communication of vibrations; the player uses the bow with one hand at a point not very far from the nut, while the notes are formed by the fingers of the other hand placed on the strings between the bow and the bridge. The notes thus produced must therefore have been all harmonics of the prime note of the string.

Judging by the information which is available concerning the education of the violin-makers of Brescia, it is impossible to avoid the suspicion that the design of the " Trompetta marina " came from some more erudite source; the same may be said of the sound-post, whether it was derived from the above-mentioned instrument or not.

In this, as in the subject about to be considered, the great influence of the Church of Rome, through members of her monastic

V.   1

institutions who were students of the arts and sciences, cannot be ignored.

As far as it is possible to judge from the instruments which are still in existence, the evolution of the varnish in which the violins were clothed appears to have followed with equal steps that of form and construction.

From existing descriptions, and from coloured illustrations, it is comparatively easy to form a conception of the varnish in its different stages without any very extensive acquaintance with the instruments themselves. Its general characteristics were manifestly persistent.

There is a consensus of opinion that the varnish is that commonly known as an " oil-varnish." To this opinion, however, there is a notable exception: M. Fétis describes the varnish of J. P. Maggini (working about 1590—1640) as a " spirit-varnish "—" la plupart " de ces instruments sont vernis à l'esprit-de-vin, d'une belle " couleur brun clair. Ce vernis est remarquable par sa finesse."* (Vol. V. 400.) A reason for this divergence will be hereafter suggested.

The earliest instruments of Brescia and Cremona were of a brown colour; although the later examples of Maggini are described and represented as inclining more towards yellow and orange, a brown tint always prevails. Among the later instruments of Cremona, Rome and other Italian cities, a recrudescence of this brown colour or tint is often to be observed.

As the form and workmanship of the violins improved, the varnish gradually exhibited purer tints of yellow and orange, brown shades became more rare, until the warm tones of Stradivari and his contemporaries appeared towards the end of the seventeenth century.

From this time until the quality of the varnish began to decline, these tints of orange and red prevailed among the Cremonese and Venetian makers.

About the year 1750, the varnish which the violin-makers had used for more than two centuries almost entirely disappeared,

---

* The greater part of these instruments are varnished with a spirit varnish, of a fine light-brown colour. This varnish is remarkable for its fine quality.

leaving no trace of its mode of manufacture. A few rare examples appeared a little later (before the close of the eighteenth century); these are supposed to have been produced at the solicitation of noble clients of the violin-maker (Guadagnini).

Apart from colour, the quality of this unrivalled varnish, the composition of which is now unknown, is excellent in every respect. When dry it still remains slightly soft, and is always elastic. If the wood on which it was spread was not perfectly seasoned at the time of its application, when the grain rose the varnish neither cracked nor fissured—it followed the most minute undulations of the wood.

For the sake of brevity, the varnishes of Brescia and Cremona will be spoken of as Cremonese. The varnish of Venice is described as very similar to that of Cremona. It is not certain that experts are capable of distinguishing the one from the other; it will be designated as Venetian.

It has been observed that some of the varnish of Stradivari is a little harder (more inclined to chip) than the generality of the Cremonese (Hill's "Stradivari," 174). It would have been interesting had the information on this point been more definite, especially if the dates and colour of the instruments possessing this peculiarity had been noted.

At some undefined period after the varnishes already mentioned had reached their zenith, varnish of a slightly different character was introduced by the violin-makers of Naples, Bologna, &c. It is less transparent than the earlier varieties when of a red colour, and, generally speaking, is not so soft or elastic. Much of it is yellow in colour, some of it red, of a deeper tint than the warmest tones of the Cremonese or Venetian varieties. This varnish will be called Neapolitan to distinguish it.

For a century the modes of preparation of these varnishes— Cremonese, Venetian, Neapolitan—have been lost. Violin-makers, chemists, amateurs, all sorts and conditions of men, have in vain attempted to re-discover the secret.

Apparently, from superficial observation, an opinion was soon formed among experts that the old varnishes were coloured, that is to say, that they all consisted of a similar or common basis tinted by the introduction of adventitious, substantive colouring matters, according to the taste of the different makers. This natural deduction from appearances has been reiterated with so much confidence, by persons having an extensive practical knowledge of the old instruments, that it has hitherto been generally accepted.

To produce successful imitations, however, in accordance with this view of their constituents, was by no means easy, owing to the difficulties attending the admixture of colouring matters with oil-varnish: organic pigments being practically insoluble in oil of turpentine and in linseed-oil.

These difficulties were in a great measure surmounted by means discovered by M. Eugène Mailand, an educated amateur, who published a book on the subject in Paris in 1859. There can be little doubt that this treatise is the foundation of all the most successful methods which have been used in modern times for the imitation of the old varnishes, although its influence has not, at all times, been acknowledged.

It has been found that these imitations do not possess the peculiar optical properties of the original substance, neither have the instruments covered with them qualities of tone similar to those of the old ones. It is supposed that these acknowledged defects are to be attributed to the want of the beneficial effects of time and use on the wood of which the violins are made as well as on the varnish in which they are clothed.

Although for a number of years, several excellent old Italian instruments had been in my possession, it must be confessed that the varnish question did not attract my attention. For more than forty years I accepted, like the rest of the world, without question or demur, the dogma which emanated from experts in whose knowledge and judgment I placed unlimited confidence. This apathy may be excused by the consideration that a coloured varnish, a mere concoction, is totally devoid of scientific interest.

Suspicion of the general soundness of the established dogma was, quite unexpectedly, aroused by the examination (in May, 1900) of a red varnish of the Neapolitan variety, which was discerned to be distinctly dichröic.

The significance of this observation was not immediately apparent, but, after some consideration of the matter, means were taken to obtain access to a number of Stradivari's instruments, of undoubted authenticity. The varnish of these was found to exhibit the same dichröic properties—red tints were evidently optical effects, the apparent colour was in no case due to substantive colouring matter or pigment.

The scientific term " dichröism " appears to have been primarily used " to denote the property exhibited by many double-refracting " crystals, of exhibiting different colours when viewed in different " directions " (Watts' Dic. of Chemistry, 1869, Vol. II. 320); Berthelot used it in 1853, 1854, to denote some such (unexplained) property in some terpene derivatives (Ann. de Chim. Vols. 38, 39, 40). It is here used to denote that the colour of transmission (yellow) differs from that of refraction (red, rarely purple).

The problem now presented was totally different from that of the skilful concoction of a coloured varnish; a research was instituted with a view to its solution. The results so far obtained are deemed of sufficient scientific interest to be worthy of publication.

The direction of the experiments was influenced by close observation of terpene derivatives to be found in different kinds of wood and in other arboreal products, many of which exhibited dichröism, due consideration being given to the physiology of the various organs of trees and the probable chemical action of the cells of which they are composed. The processes employed were intended to be imitations of those of Nature.

The extent of progress in the desired direction could only be estimated by the somewhat slow and laborious process of varnishing slips and panels of wood; eventually, for the same purpose, violins, violas, and violoncellos, of the best quality of wood and workmanship, were covered with the varnishes.

As was expected, after many months of study and experiment, it was found that every variety of the old varnishes could be reproduced with facility from turpentine and linseed-oil without the admixture of colouring matter in any form. The conclusion arrived at is that the old types were pure oil-varnishes, consisting of terpene oxides (more or less dehydrated) dissolved in linseed-oil (oxidized to varying degrees), finally diluted with oil of turpentine; in the oldest forms the linseed-oil was probably omitted.

In order that the question may be understood in all its bearings, it is necessary that a large amount of information should be given. By lay readers this must be studied with some attention, if they desire to be in a position to form a judgment on the evidence.

In the first place, descriptions of the varnishes will be gathered from many sources; arguments in favour of the theory of coloured varnishes, especially those of M. Mailand, will be quoted and criticised.

Secondly, an attempt will be made to elucidate the interesting question of the influence of varnish on tone.

Thirdly, technical information relating to the preparation of oil-varnish, derived from the most competent authorities, will be presented.

Fourthly, the preparation of dichröic oil-varnishes will be described.

Fifthly, a chapter will be devoted to the consideration of a few points relating to the chemistry of varnish and its constituents which have arisen during the progress of the experiments.

Lastly, the whole case will be summed up, and the evolution of dichröic varnishes, in my hands, will be compared with that of the olden time.

For convenience of reference, and for the benefit of readers who may desire to pursue the subject further or read for themselves the authors quoted, a list of books is given; those more directly bearing on the questions involved are marked by an asterisk(*). It is not suggested that this list approaches completeness.

CHAPTER 2

DESCRIPTIONS OF THE OLD VARNISHES—MODERN OPINIONS
AND IMITATIONS

It is not a little surprising that, among the many descriptions of the appearance of the old varnishes, only one can be said to be perfectly correct; this was given by a violinist, not by an expert. It is to be found in Fétis' book (Vol. I. 82). Writing of the violins made by Andreas Amati (who was alive and working about 1550), M. Fétis writes:—" Cartier, qui a vu deux de ces violons, affirme " que rien ne surpasse la perfection de leur travail. Ils étaient " revêtus d'un vernis à l'huile d'un ton doré, avec des reflets d'un " brun rougeâtre."* The Cartier here referred to was Jean Baptiste Cartier, born at Avignon, May 28, 1765, who came to Paris in 1783, where he became a pupil of Viotti, afterwards violinist to Marie-Antoinette. He died in Paris in 1841. The violins in question formed part of the Royal collection—" les vingt-quatre violons " du Roi "—so frequently mentioned in history.

This is an undoubted description of a dichröic varnish.

For another description which approaches this for correctness of observation, we are indebted to M. J. Gallay, editor of the new edition of the Abbé Sibire's book. The observer is again not an expert, but a violoncellist. M. Gallay writes (179) with reference to certain violoncellos, made by Antonio Stradivari, which were then in Madrid (the translation is mine):—" One of these basses, " according to the account which has been given to us by a French " artiste, M. de Try, a distinguished violoncellist, who has had, " during a tolerably long residence in Madrid, the good fortune " to play on these instruments, seems to us to be truly unique. " It is a specimen of the great period (1725); the varnish, of a fine " bright red, comes out brilliantly on a first coat of amber yellow " (" le vernis, d'un beau rouge vif, ressort brillamment sur une " première couche jaune ambré ").

---

* Cartier, who saw two of these violins, affirms that nothing could surpass the perfection of their workmanship. They were clothed in an oil-varnish of a golden tone, with reflections of reddish brown.

Here again is an unmistakable description of dichröism.

The opinion and descriptions of our own countryman, Mr. George Hart, will next be given, taken from his well-known book. At page 36 *et seq.*, Mr. Hart expresses the opinion that, " although " quite separable in one particular, which is, the depth of their " colouring, the Brescian, Cremonese, and Venetian have, to all " appearance, a common basis." In examining the Brescian varnish he finds " an almost complete resemblance between the " material of Gaspard di Salo and that of his coadjutors, the " colouring only being different." " Upon turning to the Cremonese, " we find that Joseph Guarnerius, Stradiuarius, Carlo Bergonzi, " and a few others used varnish having the same characteristics, " but, again, different in shade." He describes " the Brescian as " mostly of a rich brown colour and soft texture, but not so clear " as the Cremonese. The Cremonese is of various shades, the " early instruments of the school being chiefly amber-coloured, " afterwards deepening into light red of charming appearance, " later still into a rich brown of the Brescian type, though more " transparent." " The Venetian is also of various shades, chiefly " light red, and exceedingly transparent. The Neapolitan varnish " (a generic term including that of Milan and a few other places) " is very clear, and chiefly yellow in colour, but wanting the dainty " softness of the Cremonese."

Excluding the Neapolitan, Mr. Hart looks upon the famous varnishes as having a common basis, coloured according to the taste and skill of the individual makers. This is a very natural conception: it forms the preponderating idea which induces his theories as to the origin, evolution and disappearance of the varnishes. As to the notion that " the varnish was composed of " a particular gum quite common in those days, extensively used " for other purposes besides the varnishing of violins," reference will hereafter be made to it when the same suggestion is expressed in more confident terms by M. Mailand.

The following remarks on the varnishes of different makers are selected from those which appear in Mr. Hart's book:—

" Amati, Antonius and Hieronymus, sons of Andrew, 1570—1635. " The varnish on the earlier specimens is deeper in colour than

" that found on the later ones, which have varnish of a beautiful
" orange tint, sparingly laid on, and throwing up the markings of
" the wood with much distinctness."

" Amati, Nicholas, 1596—1684. The bellies are of a soft, silken
" nature, and usually of even grain. A few of them are of singular
" beauty, their grain being of a mottled character, which, within
" its transparent coat of vanish, flashes light here and there with
" strange force."

" Bergonzi, Carlo, 1718—1755. It is sometimes seen to be
" extremely thick, at other times but sparingly laid on; often of
" a deep, rich red colour, sometimes of a pale red, and again, of
" rich amber, so that the variation of colour to be met with in
" Bergonzi's violins is considerable. We must conclude that his
" method of varnishing was scarcely so painstaking as that of his
" fellow-workers, if we may judge from the clots here and there,
" particularly on the deep-coloured instruments; but, nevertheless,
" now that age has toned down the varnish, the effect is good."

" Guarnerius, Andreas, Cremona, 1630—1695. The varnish is
" much varied, but is generally of a light orange colour of beautiful
" hue; it sometimes has a considerable body, but when so, lacks
" the transparency of light-coloured varnishes."

" Guarnerius, Petrus, Cremona and Mantua, 1690—1728. The
" varnish is superb. Its quality is of the richest description, and
" its transparency unsurpassed. Its colour varies; it is sometimes
" of a golden tint, sometimes of a pale red, on which the light
" plays with delightful variety."

" Guarnerius, Joseph Anthony, better known as Giuseppe del
" Jesu, Cremona, 1683—1745. In some cases the lustre of the
" wood of the backs, set in its chasing of deep amber, that unrivalled
" varnish, may be likened to the effect produced by the setting
" sun on cloud and wave." Mr. Hart here quotes Byron's
description of sunset in " Childe Harold." " The varnish on such
" instruments is of a rich golden hue, highly transparent; it is
" lightly laid on."

" Stradiuarius, Antonius, Cremona, 1644—1737. The varnish on
" the instruments belonging to the period under consideration
" (1686—1694) is very varied. Sometimes it is of a rich golden

"colour, deliciously soft and transparent; in other instances he
" has used varnish of a deeper hue, which might be described as
" light red, the quality of which is also very beautiful." . . . " The
" splendour of the wood is unsurpassed in any violin, ancient or
" modern, and it was named the ' Dolphin ' from the richness and
" variety of the tints it gives to the varnish."

In spite of his theory of coloured varnishes, it is manifest that
the colour effects which he describes are those of dichröism. In
other respects, the truth and significance of Mr. Hart's excellent
descriptions will be hereafter apparent.

M. Fétis, writing of Antoine Stradivari, represents him, up to
1670, as working under the influence of Nicholas Amati; from
1670 to 1690 as more occupied in experiments and meditations on
the perfecting of his art than in making instruments for sale. In
1690 came an epoch of transition—" His varnish is more coloured."
From 1700 to 1725, the instruments which leave his hands are so
many perfect works—" Le bois, choisi avec le discernement le plus
" fin, réunit à la richesse des nuances toutes les conditions de
" sonorité. Les beaux tons chauds du vernis de Stradivarius
" datent de cette époque: la pâte en est fine et d'une grande
" souplesse.*   From 1725 to 1730 the varnish is more brown."

Another writer who is deservedly much esteemed as an authority
on the Violin is M. Antoine Vidal. He was a friend of the late
M. J. B. Vuillaume, the well-known instrument maker of Paris,
who, together with M. Georges Chanot, saw most of the instruments
which Louis Tarisio brought annually from Italy, from about the
year 1827 onwards. When Tarisio died, in 1854, M. Vuillaume
bought of his heirs the (about) 250 violins, &c. which he had accu-
mulated. Among these were some of the finest instruments in
existence. The dealers and connoisseurs of Paris, at that time,
must have enjoyed unusual opportunities for studying many fine
instruments, in their original condition.

Much of what M. Vidal writes about the varnish will be translated
and abbreviated; when his remarks are of considerable importance

* The wood, chosen with the finest discrimination, unites to richness of shades
all the conditions of sonorousness. The beautiful warm tones of the varnish of
Stradivarius date from this period. Its body is fine and of great elasticity.

they will be quoted in his own words. He is of opinion that the varnish has certainly an influence on the tone. If, on the one hand, it ought to have sufficient solidity and durability for the purposes of preservation, it must, on the other hand, possess such elasticity as to allow the parts of the instrument which it covers perfect liberty of movement; without that, it would act as a mute.

He repeats the old story of the necessity for making a basis varnish with gums of the proper degree of hardness, and then colouring it with sandal wood, dragon's blood, &c., &c. The colouring is of less importance, although demanding much care. " All that offers great difficulties, because, in the trials (experi-" ments), the greater part of the substances treated together often " do not agree, and everything has to be begun over again."

Spirit varnishes have been tried; it is said that Louis Guersan, pupil of Boquay, was the first French maker to use it. It had the great advantage of drying quickly, a few days sufficing for varnishing an instrument. But the varnish encased the instrument as if with a carapace—sonorousness was wanting. These varnishes had to be abandoned.

M. Vidal speaks with great praise of the researches of M. Eugène Mailand, which became public knowledge in 1859. In a footnote he makes the following interesting statement:—" Our great " ' luthier,' M. J. B. Vuillaume, has affirmed to us that this book of " M. Mailand had completely modified his ideas on varnish, and " that from that time he had made important changes in his method. " It is easy to convince oneself of this by examining the instruments " which left his hands during the last fifteen years of his life. The " varnish is incontestably superior to all that he had made before."

M. Vidal further writes:—" Among the old Italian masters, " A. Stradivari is the one who, from this point of view, as from " many others, has reached the greatest cleverness and perfection; " his varnish is a model both in respect to its colour as well as to its " fine and transparent body. That of Joseph Guarneri del Jesu, " when it is examined attentively, seems to be a little thicker; but " it differs above all in the nuance (hue), which is deeper. We " shall see further on, that the pupils of Stradivari commenced, in " this respect, to wander from his principles."

" Carlo Bergonzi, among others of whom we shall soon have
" occasion to speak, employed a varnish sensibly more heavy, and
" which has given to certain of his instruments that crusted appear-
" ance, much appreciated by amateurs, but which, in reality, is the
" beginning of decline (commence la décadence). New resins are
" already employed, and starting from this epoch, that is to say,
" towards 1750, the methods of the great masters begin to be
" completely lost. As we have said, the progress of the (varnish)
" industry makes itself felt; the better will kill the good."

M. Vidal afterwards speaks of the violoncellos of Carlo Bergonzi:
" with their wood so admirably chosen, their red-brown (rouge-brun)
" varnish a little thick, crackelled, but nevertheless pleasing to the
" eye."

He speaks of the varnish of Jean Paul Magini as being " of a light
brown yellow (brun jaune clair)."

After a very long search, a copy of the reprint (1874) of M.
Mailand's book was at last secured. I quite concur with M. Vidal
in his estimation of it. Although I find myself unable to agree
with M. Mailand's reasoning and his conclusions, it is readily
admitted that this work stands alone as an honest and praiseworthy
attempt to solve the mystery surrounding the old varnishes; an
attempt which must have required a large amount of labour and
patience.

M. Mailand writes (9):—" We have already said that the art of
" making varnishes at the epoch when the great masters lived was
" in a nascent state. Nevertheless, we are certain that they
" employed those which they found in commerce and which they
" appropriated to their wants. It is this which explains to us why
" these also have sometimes changed, when new formulæ were
" produced. But if they have left one formula for another, they
" have always remained under the conditions of elasticity, which
" they had recognized as necessary. As to the colouration, it has
" little effect on the quality of the varnish as body (elle importe peu
" à la qualité du vernis comme pâte), if one may so express oneself;
" and if they have often varied in this respect, that could only
" depend on the demand of the buyer, on their taste, or on the more
" or less solidity of the colouring matters."

M. Mailand gives no evidence whatever in support of his certainty that the old masters used varnishes which they found in commerce. I agree that the " conditions of elasticity " remained practically constant, for the simple reason that the constitution of the varnish was the same from start to finish. As to his astonishing statement that the colouring matter would have little effect on the quality of the varnish (" comme pâte "), I am sorry to differ from him. The very large proportion of pigment which is required to be mixed with a pale, soft resin to produce a deep-coloured varnish has a most important and deleterious effect on the quality of the body of the varnish.

He repeats, on page 12, that he " is well convinced that they (the " violin-makers) could not have employed other than the varnishes " then known in industry." " Then," he fixes as between the years 1550 and 1740.

He then gives receipts published by Alexis, the Piedmontese (" Secrets des Arts ") in 1550; by Fioravanti in 1564; by Auda in 1663; by Zahn in 1685; by Morley (Christopher) in 1692; by Coronelli in 1693; by Pomet in 1694; by Bonanni in 1713. As to the latter, he writes:—" We have found there precious information " which will allow us to conclude with certainty." (" Nous y " avons trouvé de précieux renseignements qui nous permettront de " conclure avec certitude ").

To conclude what with certainty ? Presumably what he has already set forth—that the great masters employed varnishes which were well known, at least to be found, in commerce. As this statement has been made by other writers besides M. Mailand, it will be necessary to ascertain if he produces any evidence to substantiate it; for assuredly if he does not, no other writer does.

It is submitted that what he has to do is to prove that a varnish was known in commerce which resembled that of the earliest masters of Brescia, at the time that they lived (manifestly common know-ledge in 1713 would not be relevant to Gasparo da Salo and Maggini); further, that the violin-makers improved or changed their methods as the knowledge or experience of the outside world progressed. A literal translation of his own words is repeated:—" They employed " those which they found in commerce, and which they appropriated

" to their wants. It is this which explains to us why these also " have sometimes changed when new formulæ were produced."

The formulæ quoted from the several authors are of little interest in relation to the contention which has been so confidently put forward by M. Mailand. Before endeavouring to trace a Cremonese varnish among these very crude prescriptions, some definite conception must, of necessity, be formed of the constitution of such a varnish. To avoid any difficulty on this point M. Mailand shall be met on his own ground; here is his prescription for a Cremonese varnish (156):—

" Mastic in tears   ...   .   10 grammes
" Soft Dammar (' Dammar friable ')   ...   ...   5 grammes
" Essence, coloured according to one of the for-
        mulæ already given   ...   .   100 cub cent."

The coloured essence prescribed in this formula requires some explanation. Having fixed on his resins and determined that they must be dissolved in oil of turpentine (not in alcohol), M. Mailand then proceeds to the question of colouration. He found that the colouring matters which he desired to incorporate could not be dissolved in oil of turpentine (essence). On the other hand, they were freely soluble in alcohol. But on mixing such an alcoholic solution with oil of turpentine, the two solvents refused to combine. To get over this difficulty, M. Mailand exposed oil of turpentine to air and light for six or eight weeks; it became oxygenated and resinous, much more soluble in alcohol than the original, newly-distilled oil of turpentine; this he calls " fat essence " (" essence grasse "). In this fat turpentine or " essence grasse " he dissolved his mastic and dammar, and to this solution he added his alcoholic solution of gamboge, sandal-wood, dragon's blood, &c. Having incorporated this mixture as well as possible, he proceeded to distill off or evaporate a good deal of the alcohol (he appears to have imagined that he eliminated the whole of it, in which he was mistaken).

It is quite safe to assert, beyond all chance of contention, that there is not the least indication of the preparation of " essence grasse," of any such concoction or process, in the several writers quoted; neither in Alexis, Fioravanti, Auda, Zahn, Morley, Coronelli, Pomet, or Bonanni. Whatever credit is due for the ingenuity in producing this varnish, is due to M. Mailand. To assert, on the evidence presented, that this varnish was to be found in commerce at or before the time of Bonanni (1713), is to asseverate that which cannot possibly be sustained.

M. Mailand came to his task with a settled conviction that the violin-makers used a varnish which was an article of commerce in their time. How he acquired this idea there is no evidence to shew. But his practice exhibited a good deal of common sense; he ascertained, from contemporary writers on the subject of varnish, what materials the violin-makers had at their disposal; applying modern methods to the concoction of these, he attempted to produce varnish similar to theirs.

If the authors whose works he perused knew the varnish which the violin-makers used, it might have been expected that they would have given a receipt for this special prupose, as they did in other cases:—*e.g.*, Alexis No. 2, " To give fine lustre to paintings "; No. 3, " To make a liquid to be used to varnish paintings "; Fioravanti No. 8, " This varnish is applied to skins "; No. 10, " Turkish varnish, which is also used to varnish sheet-iron and for " printers." Why is there no mention of " varnish for violin- " makers " or " for the makers of musical instruments " ? Why does not M. Mailand point out the particular prescriptions on which he relies for the support of his theory ?

It very often happens that the evidence sought is not the evidence obtained; so in this case, although M. Mailand did not get the evidence which he sought, he is good enough to give me some evidence which I wanted:—

The majority of the authors were members of the Church of Rome—" les Pères " Auda, Zahn, Morley, Coronelli, " le R. P. " (révérend père) " Bonanni, Jésuite.

Alexis (Piémontais), writing in 1550, in his No. 7 says, " and " cook the whole for the space of one hour in the water-bath (au " bain-marie) in a vessel of glass well corked."

This certifies that the water-bath and its use were known as early as 1550.

Fioravanti (Bologna, 1564) writes of linseed-oil (for its conversion to a boiled oil):—" The most common way is to boil the oil until " it burns the vanes of a feather dipped into it; some add a crust " of bread, according to the quantity of oil which they are treating, " because it absorbs its grease and makes it more easy to dry."
Boiled linseed-oil was evidently known before 1564.
Fioravanti, in the formula quoted as No. 11,

Linseed-oil	1 part
Greek pitch (*i.e.*, resin from the fir-trees of Calabria)	2 parts
Pine resin	½ part

writes, " boil until the varnish is viscous."

It was therefore known in 1564 that continued heating causes resinous substances dissolved in linseed-oil to undergo change of viscosity, probably of colour.

Father Zahn (" Oculus Artificialis," 1685) again prescribes the " bain-marie."

From Alexis we further learn that, in 1550, he used, to make varnish, " pine resin fat and white " (? galipot), " turpentine of " Venice," linseed-oil, as well as what he calls varnish of amber, which M. Mailand explains to be " a mixture of oil and of Greek pitch, which is the produce of the fir-trees (sapins) of Calabria."

It will be observed, from all the prescriptions, how much the old varnish-makers used the resins from the pine and fir-trees, as well as Venice turpentine (from larch).

The gums Alexis knew were benzoin, mastic, male incense, sandarac. For colouring, he mentions aloes, red sandal-wood, dragon's blood, madder steeped in tartar water, Campechy and Brazil wood, all dissolved in barber's ley, to which alum must be added, afterwards boiled down. Speaking of the " fastness " of colours, he adds:—" Linseed-oil kills the semi-mineral colours, " but not the mineral and vegetable." The amount of his knowledge on colouring varnishes may be estimated from this and from the fact that he prescribes cinnabar and orpiment (mercuric sulphide and arsenious sesquisulphide).

M. Mailand writes (71):—" But, it may be said to us, the " Cremonese ' luthiers ' perhaps had the secret of a varnish which

" was not in commerce and which has been lost with them. To
" that we reply, that we well understand that a person may have
" been able, doing better than his competitors, to have a secret,
" which he has carried away with him in dying; but that it is
" not supposable for an instant that a thing which has existed
" for more than a century, and which is transmitted during several
" generations of luthiers, could remain secret. It must necessarily
" be known to everybody, and has only been abandoned at the
" moment when considerable progress is made in the manufacture
" of varnishes. If it is objected that there are differences in the
" varnish of such and such a master, it is possible; but that would
" only prove one thing, which is that some knew better how to
" appropriate and employ them than others. These nuances
" make themselves felt, for the rest, more in the colour than in the
" varnishes themselves, which were all composed of tender resins.
" It is easy to be convinced of this. It is only necessary to rub
" violins of this epoch with spirit of wine; there is not one that will
" resist; if this operation is repeated on objects varnished with
" fat, hard copal varnishes which are made to-day, they cannot
" be moved."

It is agreed that the old varnishes were soluble to some extent
in alcohol; that they were not " fat, hard copal varnishes."

" As to the colours which they put into the varnish, they are
" so very transparent or translucent (tellement translucides) and
" allow the grain of the wood so well to be seen (laissent si bien
" lire la veine du bois), that we do not doubt that they employed
" resins or resinous colouring matters (! ! !). It is impossible for
" us to say by what means they managed to dissolve these in the
" essences " (*i.e.*, oil of turpentine or of aspic), " but the means is
" indifferent; what matters, is to succeed, and we have managed
" to mix them so intimately in the oils, that they do not abandon
" them again after they have been incorporated."

At page 91, M. Mailand writes:—" Essence of turpentine, it is
known, does not combine or mix with any kind of colour, whether
" ground up in oil, pulverized or distempered in the varnish; it
" is the same with the essences of lavender, aspic, or rosemary,
" —they are tinted a little more, but so feebly that they do not

v.   2

" leave any colouration when laid on." Consequently, he gets
the colour into the varnish by the medium of alcohol; it does not
matter how he gets it in so long as he succeeds.

M. Mailand observed what I also observed, although we draw
different conclusions from our observations. If a varnish were
coloured red, it would be always red, however thin the pellicle;
but he noticed that a thin pellicle was not red but yellow. He
writes (85):—" Preoccupied by the yellow tone which is met with
" on many of the instruments of the Italian luthiers, when the
" varnish is worn away, we have thought that they sized them with
" resinous gums soluble in alcohol, such as gamboge and aloes,
" which, it is said, has the property of preserving wood from
" becoming worm-eaten. These resins dissolved in alcohol are an
" excellent size, which cannot interfere with the liberty of the
" tables, nor the desiccation of the wood, since the alcohol evaporates
" at once."

M. Mailand easily smooths over missing links in his evidence.
Here is an interesting example (93):—" Alexis does not speak of
" gamboge, which, however, was known in his time."

Having made up his mind to sizing as a way out of this difficulty
(the colour of the worn part being yellow, while the thicker pellicle
appeared orange or red), M. Mailand proceeds to account for the
use of size as a prelimianry coat—the instructed reader will observe
how many mistakes he makes in endeavouring to support his
theory. He writes (81):—" Is it necessary to size instruments
" before varnishing them ? We do not hesitate to reply affirma-
" tively; for if they were not sized the two or three first (sic !)
" coats of varnish would enter the wood; they would remain
" completely dull until saturation of the wood, which, not being
" able to absorb any more of it, would be sized by the varnish
" itself: this is easy to explain. The wood, by its cellular canals,
" fulfils the office of a sponge; it absorbs the most fluid part of
" the varnish, and so much the more the longer it has previously
" undergone desiccation; in consequence the instrument will be
" saturated with essence, with a proportion of resins and of
" colouring matters, of which the surplus will remain on the surface,
" at least, if the varnish is very viscid. These resins deprived of

" a portion of their essence, being left to themselves (se trouvant
" abandonnées à elles-mêmes), will dry promptly, losing the
" suppleness which it ought to communicate to them. It would
" evidently result from this way of doing, that more coats would
" be necessary to obtain the necessary brilliancy, that the varnish
" which we employ, into which no hard resins enter, would become
" very friable, since they would have lost, in part, the excipient "
(curious word ! compare Fleming 270) " which ought to protect
" them, and that to arrive at a suitable solidity, it would be
" necessary to give two or three coats more; that at length, when
" these last shall have become oxidised by time or worn by rubbing,
" those beneath will fall promptly into powder; but the most
" grave inconvenience would be, on the one hand, of having caused
" the wood to absorb a certain quantity of varnish, and on the
" other of having put on to it a thickness more considerable than
" useful; in consequence the sounds of the instrument would
" be dull, veiled, without brilliancy, and without carrying power;
" if not for ever at least for a very long space of time.   The woods
" employed in violin-making (lutherie) are not used until they
" are very dry, desiccation which can only be obtained after
" several years, from which it follows that in causing the essence
" and the resins to penetrate the wood, one would do a thing quite
" contrary to the end which one proposed to oneself to attain."

This singular and totally erroneous notion of what happens to
wood in the process of drying or seasoning, M. Mailand puts quite
clearly, at page 61:—" For in violin-making the wood which is
" the most dry is esteemed; that, in a word, which has lost its
" resin " (car on recherché en lutherie les bois les plus secs; ceux
en un mot qui ont perdu leurs resines).

It is needless to say that wood is apt to become more, rather
than less, resinous in drying; the resins which are in the fresh wood
are perfectly stable and always remain; parts of the volatile
essential oils are likely to become resinous by oxidation during the
slow, drying process.

M. Mailand's statement as to what happens to a varnish when
spread on dry wood is pure imagination; it is not so easy to dissociate
the resins from the heavier parts of the essence as he supposes.

M. Mailand is fully aware that his view—that it is necessary to prevent the wood of violins from absorbing varnish—is directly opposed to that of M. Savart.

There is one singular circumstance connected with the experiments of M. Mailand to which attention must be directed. It will be remembered that he rubbed an old Italian violin with spirits of wine in order to ascertain if the varnish were soluble in this menstruum or not. He does not say how he made this test, but it may be assumed that he moistened a piece of cotton or linen cloth with alcohol and applied it to the varnish. The varnish was soluble in alcohol; consequently a small quantity of dissolved varnish was transferred to the surface of the cloth. If M. Mailand had observed the colour of this varnish on the cloth, he would have seen that it was not the same as the apparent colour of the thick pellicle, but exactly matched that of the thin film where the varnish was worn away, which he had observed to be yellow. It is evident that if he had made this simple observation all his theories would have been scattered to the winds. Either he neglected to make the observation, or, if he made it, he was so infatuated with his preconceived ideas that he simply ignored it.

*   *   *   *   *   *

The description which the Messrs. Hill give of the Maggini varnishes on the Dumas instruments is as follows (G. P. Maggini, 63):—" The varnish of the violin is fine and abundant, and most " pleasing in colour, being of a peculiar golden yellow, subdued " in places with pale brown. It yields, when a good light plays " on it, effects delightful in their way, embodying at once the " fascinations of amber and of gems such as the sardius and topaz, " though no doubt some part of this fascination is due to changes " effected by time." Of the viola:—" Time and men have indeed " dealt kindly with this noble instrument. Not only is the wood " intact, but the varnish shows only slight signs of wear, and is " of the finest quality and most original colour, a rich golden " brown, ever ready to flash under the magic of light into colour " surprises which beggar words. In sunshine the back seems com- " pact of ' myriads of topaz lights,' touched here and there with

" gleams of purple, though here again, no doubt, time has done
" its part " (66).

This exhausts the various statements and opinions which it
appears necessary to record; I have read a great deal more, both
interesting and amusing, but, for the present purpose, I have
failed to induce myself to take seriously the views put forward
(*e.g.*, Haweis).

From these descriptions and from others to be found in the
authors quoted, a rough diagram may be constructed which may
in a general and imperfect way give a graphic idea of the movements
of the different qualities of the varnish.

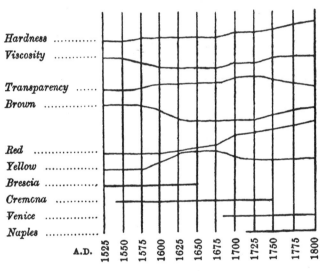

It is admitted that the generally expressed opinion, that the
different varieties of the varnish had a common basis, is well
founded. That this basis was used for other purposes is also
admitted; but this is quite a different thing from admitting that
the basis was a gum or that the special varnishes under consideration
were known in commerce or were used for other purposes, which is
explicitly denied.

All the observers, inadvertently, describe effects of colour caused
by refraction; the most striking description is that given by Mr.
Hart when he likens the appearance of the back of a violin by

Joseph Guarnerius del Jesu to " the effect produced by the setting
" summer sun on cloud and wave." " The varnish on such
" instruments is of a rich golden hue, highly transparent; it is
" lightly laid on." This simile is absolutely correct; the conditions
in the two cases assimilate very closely.

In the case of the sunset, the effects are produced by refraction
and polarization, caused by the passage of the solar rays, at a
particular angle, through the refracting medium of the atmosphere;
when cloud or precipitated moisture lies in the path of the polarized
rays, double refraction and dichröic effects ensue (in the shadows of
clouds and waves complementary colour may be often observed).
The highly refracting varnish of the violin represents its atmosphere;
the grain of the maple wood, which reflects the incident rays from
constantly varying planes, replaces the clouds. A violin is selected
of the golden hue which Mr. Hart specifies; the back is held in such
a position that the incident rays of light and a line drawn from the
observer's eye to the centre of the back are at an approximate right
angle with the curved surfaces of the varnish; this position represents mid-day; the colour of the back is yellow interspersed with
clouds of neutral colour. The angle which the longer axis of the
back forms with the eye and the direction of the light is gradually
made more obtuse; sunset approaches, warm tones slowly shew
themselves in the clouds until, finally, the back of the violin appears
to be composed of strata of red, red-brown, and yellow.

How any educated person can confuse effects such as these with
monochrome colour (even with two monochromes drawn one over
the other) passes comprehension.

Mr. Hill's description of refraction effects is almost equally good,
but he seems to be afraid to let himself go—he delineates forcibly
with one hand while with the other he holds fast to a cherished
theory.

The excellent coloured representations of a few of the ancient
instruments, for which the world is indebted to the Messrs. Hill, are
equally fatal to the monochrome theory—the artist portrays the
different thicknesses of the pellicle of varnish, the variety caused by
light and shadow, not as shades of the same colour but as distinct
colours.

As with the sunset and sunrise, so with the varnish.   Herein lies the charm—that the tints are constantly changing with varying conditions of intensity, quality and direction of light.   It is absolutely impossible to imitate these effects by coloured imitations; the notion that age will impart to these concoctions the properties of dichröic varnishes is quite illusory.

M. Mailand did one great service to M. J. B. Vuillaume and his other followers, in that he taught them to use oxygenated turpentine in forming their mixtures; curiously enough, as far as can be discovered, neither he nor they appreciated the real significance of this proceeding.

CHAPTER 3

THE TONE OF VIOLINS

THE question whether the quality of the varnish applied to the wood of which violins (generic) are constructed has any decided influenced on their tone, must be, without any hesitation, answered in the affirmative.

The wood of which these instruments are made is of a light and absorbent character: it consists largely of sclerogen, without much encrusting or agglutinating matter. The wood of the belly, or table, which receives the primary impulse of vibration, through the medium of the bridge, is of the very lightest description that can be procured; at the same time, it is selected of regular and even grain.

Apart from the question of appearance and protection, to some extent, from climatic and other deteriorating influences, it is generally admitted that an unvarnished violin will not permanently possess the necessary qualities for the production of good tone.

M. Antoine Vidal (whose opinion, it may be surmised, was based, to a great extent, on the experience of his friend, M. Vuillaume) writes thus (the translation is mine):—" Experience replies clearly " to these questions: the violin finished and not varnished has more " power and mellowness in its tone; but if it remains in this virgin " state, it becomes modified little by little, and, after a somewhat " short time, the tone becomes poor and feeble. It must therefore " be concluded that the varnish, while giving a more pleasing " appearance, conserves, preserves, and that therein, above all, " consists its great utility."

The Abbé Sibire (who spoke for Nicholas Lupot) expressed a similar opinion (75).

The concurrence of M. Félix Savart with this view will, a little later, be quoted at length.

The table of a violin (the back also in a somewhat auxiliary sense) is intended to be a diaphragm which, receiving its vibratory impulse from the strings, through the bridge, communicates the vibrations to the air contained in the instrument.

In order to fulfil the delicate functions required, such a diaphragm must possess a certain amount of homogeneity, its component fibres must not be susceptible of independent motion or vibration; it must be sufficiently elastic to respond to the slightest impulse, but its resistance must give rise to vigorous reaction.

In trying to understand this complex problem, let an extreme case be supposed: a diaphragm is constructed of unsized paper, *i.e.*, of practically pure cellulose in the form of interlaced, elongated cells. Vibration communicated to this diaphragm will be disseminated among the fibres of which it is composed, the motion will be individual instead of combined; as a diaphragm it will be a failure.

Saturate this diaphragm with a varnish which, when dry, will render it homogeneous and elastic, it will now respond to the most delicate vibration; no impulse will be strong enough to cause individual motion among its fibres. The brilliancy of the tone produced will, of necessity, depend on the resistance which this elastic diaphragm offers to the vibrations which are communicated to it; for action and reaction are equal and opposite. This resistance will mainly depend on the physical attributes of the varnish with which the fibrous diaphragm is impregnated.

Again, instead of saturating the paper so thoroughly as to cause perfect homogeneity, let it be supposed that the varnish is diluted, in order that the impregnation may be partial, not complete, so far as the ultimate constituents of the varnish (minus the vehicle) are concerned; the diaphragm will now vibrate, as when completely saturated, under the influence of a gentle impulse, but if the amplitude or repetition of the vibrations be carried beyond a certain point, the fibres now being only lightly agglutinated, an individual motion will be caused, as well as the combined one. This is, apparently, the effect intended to be described when an instrument is said to be overplayed.

This latter supposed condition of the imaginary diaphragm represents roughly the finished, unvarnished violin. It will be easily conceived that, if the fibres of the wood be only lightly agglutinated, any long-continued vibration will have a tendency to cause increasing dislocation (a slipping of one fibre on the other)— individual motion instead of combined movement. This dislocation may be permanent or temporary.

If the old instruments be carefully examined, it will be found that not only did the varnish cover the wood, but it saturated its outer layer, thus forming a homogeneous and elastic diaphragm such as has been described. The outer stratum of the wood (forming table, back, and ribs) is no longer soft and porous, it is homogeneous and compact; in fact, after all the surface varnish has been worn away, the bare wood takes a fine polish; it is clearly to be discerned that the varnish has penetrated the wood to some depth.

Mr. Edward J. Payne, author of the article on Antonio Stradivari in Grove's " Dictionary of Music," writes thus of Stradivari's varnish:—" It is oil varnish of a soft and penetrating nature, " apparently permeating the wood to some depth beneath the " surface, so that when the body of the varnish is worn off the " colour and substance appear to remain."

Probably no one has made so many experiments on the tone of instruments as the late M. Félix Savart, of Paris. His opinion is thus quoted by M. Mailand (46) (the translation is mine):—" The " varnish adds to the beauty at the same time that it renders the " quality of sound permanent; when the varnishing of the table is " neglected, the instrument loses its mellowness and its force. No " one is ignorant that guitars whose tables are not varnished lose " much with age; it is the same with pianofortes. It might be " thought that in this latter instrument, the deterioration, after " some years of service, would depend entirely on the considerable " pressure exerted on the table by the tension of the multiplicity of " strings; but it derives its origin from another source. If it " depended only on the cause which has been assigned to it, the " sound would not become acute or shrill (aigu) and meagre (maigre) " as it does become: it would become dull (sourd = deaf) and " feeble (faible), as I have had reason to remark (or observe) that " it does when I made violins of which the tables were too thin, or " to which I fixed no bar; they became dull (sourd) in proportion

"' to the sinking of the table, and never meagre. It appears that in
" pianofortes the vibrations communicated to the table by a great
" number of strings which vibrate harmonically with the principal
" sound (prime note), destroy little by little the texture (contexture)
" of the wood, with the expulsion of a great number of particles in
" the form of dust; for if the firwood which has been used in a
" pianoforte is wrought, it appears to be very porous and as if
" rotten. It is presumable that the humidity of the air counts for
" a good deal in this change of its nature: for violins do not
" deteriorate, although much pressed by the tension of their strings,
" while guitars, which are no more pressed, deteriorate very
" promptly. It is the same with violins when they are not
" varnished: the sound has at first more mellowness and force than
" if they had been varnished; but it becomes modified little by
" little, and at length feeble and meagre, which happens in a
" tolerably short time."

M. Savart is further quoted (58):—" In general the violins are
" most esteemed which are covered with an oil varnish " (*i.e.*, a
varnish whose vehicle is oil of turpentine). " I believe well enough
" that this is with reason, since it is more adhesive than that which
" is made with spirit of wine; it is more suitable for instruments of
" which the tables are thin, because by penetrating them, it gives
" them more consistence. I think, on the contrary, that for
" violins of which the tables are thick, a better varnish is that
" which permeates less into the wood and which leaves it all its
" natural qualities. That of lac dissolved to saturation in rectified
" spirit of wine of 34 or 36 degrees has appeared to me very suitable;
" it dries promptly and is not liable to scale off." Speaking of
colours, such as saffron and arnatto, he says:—" It appears that
" they have a bad effect on the wood, and contribute to make the
" sound piercing or shrill (aigre); lac varnish gives a very beautiful
" tint, to which one might hold oneself (à laquelle on pourrait se
" tenir), and which has no bad effect whatever."

M. Mailand thinks M. Savart's remarks as to the different
treatment of thin and thick tables illogical.

The question of choice of vehicle is of paramount importance.
It is obviously useless to possess a suitable resin if it simply remains

on the surface of the wood, as it would do in the spirit varnish which M. Savart proposes; if lac were soluble in oil of turpentine the position would be changed. The strong affinity which most woods possess for this latter vehicle is remarkable (not very easy to understand). The absorption of alcohol and water by wood is neither very rapid nor complete; but if a section of wood be dropped into oil of turpentine, saturation appears to be instantaneous; the wood at once becomes diaphanous, which is not the case when it has been immersed in the two other fluids for some time. Duration of evaporation is an equally important factor; alcohol leaves resin so speedily that, apart from affinity, no reasonable time is allowed for absorption.

Let us, firstly, consider the question which M. Savart raises relating to climatic influences.

It is somewhat remarkable that the relations of varnish and moisture to the wood of a violin have not been, ere now, exactly defined. Such questions may not be neglected, because eventually they may prove to be of great importance. When, during the course of these experiments, the time had arrived for testing varnish on a virgin violin (" in the white "), the first thing requisite was to accurately weigh the instrument. A coat of one of the oil-varnishes, hereafter described, was laid on with a brush; as soon as the varnish was sufficiently dry, the violin was again weighed: it weighed rather less than it did originally. This result was certainly unexpected. The same experiment was repeated with another instrument—with the same result. One of two things must have happened:—1st. The varnish had displaced from the wood something heavier than itself (? water); or 2nd. While the varnish was drying, the wood had lost more weight by elimination of moisture than it had gained by the coat of varnish.

On close investigation it was found not to be so easy to determine the exact weight of an unvarnished violin as might be supposed; the weight was never constant from one day to another. If the instrument was hung up in a room where the temperature is practically constant, at about 16° C. (60° F.), its weight changed with changes of weather which affected the hygroscopic condition of the air.

The weight of a virgin violin (without finger-board), which has been made for some years, will generally be found to be between 4,400 and 4,900 grains (say 285 to 317 grammes) at 60° F. This weight will increase or decrease to the extent of at least 60 grains (4 grammes) when the violin is exposed to the air of different apartments in the same house. If the weight of the unvarnished instrument, when in an ordinary sitting-room, be taken as 4,500 grains (300 grammes), it may be safely assumed that of this weight about 500 grains (33 grammes) are water. This considerable proportion of water present in wood (even when well dried and seasoned) makes it very difficult to determine with exactitude how much weight the virgin instrument gains by the varnishing of its exterior surfaces.

It has been found that the increase of weight in a violin by the varnishing process ranges from about 200 to 400 grains (13 to 26 grammes). The actual weight of the varnish will slightly exceed this, because it must be taken into account that the varnish which has permeated the wood has in all probability displaced an equal volume of water.

If the wood of violins were varnished on all sides there might be more reason for the conclusion at which M. Savart arrived in endeavouring to explain the reason for the greater deterioration of the sounding-boards of guitars and pianofortes than of those of violins. He appears to have overlooked the fact that the inside of a violin is unvarnished; therefore, from this direction the wood will be always freely affected by the humidity of the atmosphere.

It is easy to ascertain whether a varnished violin is so affected. A completely varnished, unmounted violin (*i.e.*, one without finger-board, tail-piece, bridge, sound-post, pegs, &c.), which has been hanging for many months in an even temperature of about 60° F., and in an atmosphere which is comparatively dry, is accurately weighed; its weight is 5,038 grains. It is removed to another apartment (in the same house) on an upper floor, where the temperature is about 10° F. less, the air more humid.

> After 24 hours its weight is 5,056 grains;
> After 48 hours its weight is 5,068 grains.

Returned to the warmer apartment it loses weight again until it reaches its normal of about 5,038 grains. Its weight will always depend upon the state of the external atmosphere. When frost sets in, its weight falls, in a few hours, below 5,000 grains; on account of the dryness of the air of the room consequent on the raising of the temperature of the cold, dry, external air which is gradually introduced, to 60° F.

I have made great numbers of careful and exact experiments on the question of the absorption of moisture by wood (new and old, seasoned and unseasoned) from the atmosphere; the weight of wood is never constant, it follows the atmospheric conditions. Even doors which are French-polished on both sides and on their edges modify their weight and dimensions with the changes of the weather and of the seasons.

It must be evident, therefore, that M. Savart was labouring under some misapprehension when he ascribed the differences in the deterioration of the tables of violins, guitars, and pianofortes to climatic influences. Manifestly, the explanation must be sought in some other direction.

Having disposed of the question of climatic influences, we have, secondly, to consider the other point which M. Savart raises by his suggestion that in an unvarnished sounding-board the vibrations destroy, little by little, the texture of the wood. It must be admitted that this proposition is presented in a somewhat loose form, even if we substitute his own word " contexture " for texture. It is not quite clear what he means, or whether he had formed any definite mental conception.

In order to obtain such an exact mental conception of the possible effect of vibrations on the structure of wood, a somewhat long digression will be unavoidable.

The cells of which trees and plants are constructed may be described (for the present purpose) as vesicles having thin membraneous walls, formed of cellulose, but in nearly all cases more or less thickened by other substances. These membranes are permeable by fluids. The forms of these cells are of infinite variety; they appear generally to be derived from spheres, spheroids, or tapered cylinders, the derived angular or irregular forms being probably dependent on the conditions to which the cells are subjected, according to their positions in various structures.

Everyone knows that a vessel or vesicle formed of a thin membrane has vastly different properties whether it is filled with a very light and elastic fluid, such as air (uncompressed), or with a comparatively dense and inelastic one, such as water; the substitution of the latter fluid for the former has a great stiffening effect on the vessel—it becomes much more rigid. In the case of the thin-walled cells of parenchyma, this may be one of the reasons for increase of rigidity, but it cannot apply to the sclerenchymatous cells of wood, which are much affected by accessions of moisture (such as absorption from the atmosphere) which are quite insufficient to fill the cells; in this case the increase in rigidity must be ascribed to that thickening of the cell-walls by the absorption of moisture which is known as turgidity.

We have before us a succulent plant constructed of cells in various forms. The tapered stem is erect; the branches are either horizontal or slightly removed from the horizontal position upwards or downwards or bending in graceful curves; attached to these branches, by appropriate stalks or petioles, are broad leaves expanded in planes approximately horizontal.

Arrangements are made to cut off the usual supply of water to the absorbent roots of the plant. Evaporation continues from the leaves until the water in the cells is dissipated in the surrounding air. The stem is now no longer able to support the weight of the organs attached to it—it bends and inclines to one side; the branches decline from their usual position; the leaves become flaccid and droop.

Water is again supplied to the roots; in a short time the plant resumes its original graceful form.

These phenomena are, of course, due to the loss and recovery by the cells of that stiffness or rigidity which has been already ascribed to the presence of water. It must be evident, however, that if each individual cell occupied an isolated position no such effect could be produced; it is essential that the cells should be firmly attached to each other by some agglutinating substance, sufficient to cause adhesion of their parts in contact, in order that individual rigidity may afford the combined strength necessary to withstand the strains of flexure and torsion to which the various parts of the plant are subjected.

The rope-maker takes a quantity of hemp, reduced, by suitable means, to long fibres composed of bundles of elongated cells attached to each other by some agglutinant. He twists numbers of these into the form of a cord. He again twists a number of these cords into a strand. From several of the strands, in a similar manner, he finally constructs the rope; which is, in fact, composed of a complicated system of fibrous spiral springs. If this new, dry rope be strained between two fixed points, the amount of its tension may be ascertained by weights or other equivalent arrangement. If the rope be now saturated with water, the tension which it exerts at the two fixed points will be largely increased. This phenomenon is again due to the stiffening or increased rigidity of the fibrous spiral springs caused by the water absorbed by the cells; in short, to turgescence, each individual cell being suitably attached or agglutinated to its fellows by a substance naturally or artificially introduced for this purpose.

Wood consists of numbers of elongated cells similarly attached to each other. If dry wood be saturated with water it will be found to change its form; it will be considerably enlarged laterally but not appreciably longitudinally—in common language, it swells. As it dries it resumes its original dimensions. This phenomenon is once more to be attributed to turgidity—to the increase and decrease of the strength or rigidity of the tiny cells, firmly attached to each other by the adhesion of parts of their membraneous walls.

Now a still more remarkable phenomenon has to be observed: If the alternate saturation and desiccation of the rope and of the wood be indefinitely repeated, it will be found that the intensity of the effects described grows gradually less and less—the longitudinal contraction of the rope, the lateral expansion of the wood, slowly but perceptibly, decreases; the rope becomes old, the wood becomes seasoned.

How is this interesting phenomenon to be explained ? Have the ultimate cells of the hemp and of the wood gradually lost the property of turgescence, of acquiring increased rigidity from the absorption of water? This seems inconceivable: fortunately we possess means of proving, beyond all doubt, that such is not the case. We take parts of the old rope and of the seasoned wood; by suitable chemical means we deprive the cells, of which these substances are mainly composed, of all extraneous matter until membranes of practically pure cellulose remain. These purified cells are suspended in sufficient water to constitute a conveniently diffuse magma; paper is made from it by two different methods, the one process being known as hand-making, the other as machine-making. In the first process, the workman dips a rectangular form (covered on the under side with fine wire gauze) beneath the surface; he raises it; as the water escapes through the gauze, by a dexterous shake he causes the fibres to cross each other or interlace at the moment when they are forming a sheet of paper. In the second process, the mixture of cellulose and water is caused to flow, in a wide, thin stream, on to a slowly, forward-moving sheet of wire gauze; this has also a lateral shaking motion which, to a certain extent, interlaces the fibres at the moment when the water is leaving them; but this interlacing is less complete than in the first process, for the current of the stream has a tendency to cause all the fibres to float in a longitudinal direction—their longer axes tend to remain in the same plane as that in which the water and the gauze are moving.

When the sheets of paper so made are sufficiently dry, they are impregnated with a resinous or colloïd substance to an extent sufficient to cause mutual adherence of the fibres without producing an impervious integument.

The hand-made paper will be (practically) equally strong in every direction; the machine-made will be much stronger longitudinally than laterally. If both kinds of paper, when dry, be again moistened, they will expand; the hand-made nearly equally in all directions, the machine-made much more laterally than longitudinally. If the alternate processes of moistening and drying be repeated, it will be found that the ratio of expansion slowly, but surely, decreases.

It is therefore perfectly clear that the ultimate fibres of the hemp and wood have retained their original attributes unchanged from first to last.

In the problem before us we had but two factors:—1st. Turgescence, the increase of rigidity caused by absorption of water; 2nd. The aggregation of effect caused by the mutual adhesion of the cells. It is submitted that clear proof has been adduced that the first factor is a constant; it follows, of necessity, that the characteristic changes in the structures, formed by the aggregation of cells, must be caused by some alteration in the second factor— their mutual adhesion.

The explanation of the observed phenomena can no longer be doubtful:—The movements of the individual fibres, caused by the strains set up by the alternate wetting and drying, must have, to some extent, modified or destroyed their mutual adhesion; by constant repetition they have acquired accommodation to the requirements of their environment, the friction of their surfaces in contact has become lessened by repeated strain or movement, they slip one on the other to the required extent.

In the case of ropes which are repeatedly subjected to complete immersion and saturation, a part of the agglutinant may have been removed by the solvent action of water; this cannot be the case with wood which is subjected only to continual changes in the hygroscopic condition of the atmosphere.

The seasoning, in the case of ropes or of pieces of wood (such as oars) which are alternately completely saturated, then partially or completely dried, will be quite different (in degree) from that of wood under shelter, exposed only to atmospheric changes. The seasoning or immunity from change of form will apply only within the limits of moisture and desiccation to which the fibrous structure has become accustomed.

If, then, the slow movements, arising from strains which are set up in wood by changes of hygroscopic conditions, are capable of gradually loosening the adhesion of the fibres to each other to a small extent, it may be expected that continual vibrations, more or less violent, will produce similar results in an aggravated form.

As wood which is of a •(so-called) mild character, *i.e.*, which contains a minimum quantity of evenly distributed agglutinating matter, will season more quickly than wood which is saturated with some resinous or adhesive substance (often so unevenly distributed as to cause cracks and fissures before the gradual accommodation to strains has had time to be perfected), so may it be expected that the influence of vibrations, in causing dislocation, disintegration, or (to use the expression of M. Savart) destruction of contexture, will be in inverse proportion to the degree of agglutination.

M. Savart states, as the result of actual experiments, that violins which are unvarnished soon deteriorate in tone. This fact appears to be confirmed by other observers; to my knowledge, the correctness of this observation has never been disputed.

When due consideration is given to all the observed facts, only one conclusion appears possible: that the deteriorating influence is vibration, which causes a kind of dislocation of the fibrous cells of the wood—they slip or move on each other without much friction or adhesion—individual motion becomes more or less possible. When varnish penetrates the wood so as to produce a practically homogeneous diaphragm, this dislocating action of the vibrations is prevented.

Most persons who are in the habit of playing on a stringed instrument with a bow will have observed that if a violin, viola, or violoncello has not been played on for some months or years the tone will not be produced at first with the same facility as after some weeks of daily use; the sounding-boards of the instrument will offer more resistance at the beginning than at the end of a period of frequent playing; there will be a perceptible difference in the tone after a period of complete rest as compared with one of daily practice—always supposing that a good instrument is in question. The Messrs. Hill, writing on this subject, express themselves very strongly (Stradivari, 239):—" To close—one most earnest word. " Instruments by continual use are apt to become weary. They " may even virtually be killed. Give them rests. We feel it a " duty to urge most strongly that fine instruments should not be " brought to premature death by ceaseless use."

Physiologists have given much study to the weariness, or decline of power of response, which overtakes living cells (animal and vegetable) under varying conditions of excitement and work. It can be no such problem which is set before us in considering the change in the condition of the dead cells of a stringed instrument caused by repeated and varied vibrations. This can be no question of exhausted vitality or of subtle electrical conditions—the change must be purely physical.

During the course of these experiments an incident occurred that throws some light on this subject. Certain violins were varnished with pure turpentine varnishes (containing no oil). After drying, for at least six weeks, it was found that if the surface of the varnish (which was not sticky) was briskly rubbed with the fingers (a cloth would not do) the surface pulverised. If this powder was carefully removed, by means of a dry cloth or brush, a dull, opaque surface of varnish would remain. After a few hours, or at most a day or two, this dull surface spontaneously regained (temp. 60° F.) its former smooth, translucent, bright appearance. This experiment was repeated with various similar varnishes with the same result.

The particles of varnish which had become disintegrated by friction regained their cohesion after a period of rest.

The belly or table of a violin is formed of a thin section of firwood (Abies or Picea). The elongated cells or fibres (interspersed with medullary rays) of which it is composed are agglutinated with a soft resin (terpene oxide), sparingly distributed. The proportion of this agglutinant is not enough to constitute with the sclerogen a diaphragm of sufficient homogeneity or endurance to resist permanently the disintegrating influence of strong musical vibrations; when subjected to these, for any length of time, the quality of the sounding-board becomes deteriorated; it does not regain its original condition after a period of rest: apparently the amount of resin present is insufficient to allow of re-cohesion.

If the exterior surface only of this sounding-board be coated with varnish of such a quality that it is able to permeate the wood to a greater or less depth, a very complex condition of this fibrous diaphragm must ensue; the exterior surface of the wood will be (it may be assumed) completely saturated, while the interior surface will not be reached by the varnish or in any way affected. Between these two extremes of complete saturation and total immunity there will be gradations of absorption, constituting zones which will offer great or little resistance to the dislocating influence of vibration. If this assumption be well founded (the recorded facts seem to leave little room for doubt), it is not difficult to conceive what will happen. The wood which has received no accession of agglutinant from the varnish, after a comparatively brief period of use, will become permanently disqualified; this disposes of the innermost zone. Next we have to consider the zone which has received from the varnish the minimum quantity of agglutinating material; by constant vibration it may be supposed that this zone also, at a little later date, will become disintegrated, at least temporarily. A similar effect will ensue, after still longer endurance, in the zones with constantly increasing increments of varnish or resin (short of sufficient to constitute homogeneity), consequently with gradually augmented power of resistance to the dislocating influence. In this way, the effect of constant playing (continued vibration) must be to gradually diminish the thickness of the effective diaphragm.

With rest (if a similar resumption of cohesion takes place within the wood as has been shown to ensue with the varnish on the surface), those zones, which have not entirely lost their power of recuperation (*i.e.*, where the amount of resin is sufficient to allow of re-cohesion), will soon resume their original condition of resistance: the violin will regain its normal state of sonorousness and brilliancy.

It seems impossible to conceive any other hypothesis which will satisfy all the conditions.

Practical experiments have confirmed these theoretical conclusions. There seems to be no doubt that not only does the production of satisfactory tone depend on the permeation of the wood by the elastic varnish with which the instrument is covered, but the particular quality of tone produced is influenced by the characteristics of the varnish which has been absorbed.

A general impression appears to prevail that the tone of instruments of the violin family improves with age. The facts on which this opinion is based are not evident. The deterioration of the tone of some instruments by use and age seems to have been satisfactorily demonstrated, but evidence of the converse is wanting. It is admitted that the tone of many old instruments, especially those of Italian origin, is generally superior to that of modern instruments, but there appears to be no sufficient reason for supposing that with age the latter will become equal to or approach the quality of the former. It would appear that during the lifetime of Stradivari the superiority of his instruments was acknowledged and appreciated. There is no evidence that the artistes and amateurs who lived at that time, and who were quite capable of forming a correct judgment on the question, preferred the older instruments of Brescia and Cremona to those which came direct from his hands (especially between 1700 and 1725).

Until real evidence is produced to the contrary, it would be more safe to assume that the old Italian instruments, which are so must esteemed to-day, owe their superiority to qualities which they have always possessed since they left the hands of their makers, or which they acquired within a year or two from the date of their completion.

Everyone who has studied Professor Helmholtz's admirable work on the " Sensations of Tone," will be aware that the distinctive qualities of tone, of human voices, and of various kinds of musical instruments, depend upon the strength of the upper partials which the ear analyses as accompanying the prime tones, thus forming compound tones made up of constituents of varying prominence. A thin string tuned to a certain pitch will produce a compound tone which will differ very considerably, in the prominence of its constituents, from that derived from a thick or covered string tuned to the same pitch.

In violins the sympathy between the strings and the belly or table is so intimate that it is impossible to conceive that a change in the varnish, which is sufficient to influence the degree of elasticity or of resistance of the vibrating diaphragm—to cause a diminution or increase of amplitude of vibration—shall be without effect on the quality of tone.

CHAPTER 4

ON THE MANUFACTURE OF OIL-VARNISH

BEFORE proceeding to attempt to describe the best known methods for the preparation of oil-varnish, it will be well to define as nearly as possible the attributes of a perfect varnish.

A varnish consists of a soluble, transparent, adhesive solid, or of a combination of such substances, dissolved in a volatile fluid which is called the "vehicle." When the vehicle evaporates, a solid pellicle remains on the surface to which the varnish has been applied. A very little consideration will make it evident that, if the best results are to be obtained this pellicle must be perfectly homogeneous; in other words, if it consists of more than one substance, its constituents must be, not in a state of intimate mixture only, but blended—actually incorporated the one with the other.

Take an oil-varnish, for instance: Copal is fused and dissolved in linseed-oil (properly prepared for the purpose); this viscid solution is then diluted with the volatile vehicle (oil of turpentine), to render it convenient of application, by means of a brush. When the vehicle evaporates spontaneously, a thin and perfectly homogeneous pellicle remains: the copal is dissolved in and incorporated with the linseed-oil. This is conceived to be a perfect varnish.

Suppose it is desired to give to an oil-varnish an artificial colour, by means of some substance which is insoluble (or only partially soluble) in linseed-oil or oil of turpentine. The pigment is dissolved in alcohol; this coloured solution is intimately mixed with the varnish. When the alcohol and the oil of turpentine evaporate, the colouring-matter is precipitated in a state of fine division in the varnish, but the pellicle is no longer homogeneous; although the colouring-matter may be distributed ever so evenly or skilfully, it is adventitious, foreign (so to speak) to the other and main constituents of the pellicle; it is not dissolved in nor incorporated with either of them. It is suggested that a varnish so constituted is manifestly imperfect.

No one who studies the existing descriptions of the manufacture of oil-varnishes can fail to be impressed by the surprising technical skill, requisite for their successful production, which has been for so long a time available. The maker of oil-varnish is an expert: a man of high intelligence, quick observation, cool judgment; prepared with ready wit and presence of mind in all emergencies. But a very little consideration will show that this important industry rests more upon the skill and experience which have grown up from long practice than upon a scientific basis or exact knowledge of cause and effect.

Among the many writers on this subject, from Professor Tingry to those of the present time, no one appears to have described the processes with more lucidity and exactness than M. Laurent Naudin. His excellent treatise forms one of the numbers of that admirable series of technical works known as the " Encyclopédie scientifique des aide-mémoire," published under the direction of M. Léauté, Membre de l'Institut.

His description of the preparation of a copal oil-varnish may be thus translated and somewhat abridged:—" The pieces of copal " are selected for colour and hardness. The great point is to " select, as nearly as possible, pieces of the gum which have the " same degree of fusibility. These selected fragments are cleaned " and dried; they are then ready for fusion."

" The softer (demi-dur) copal produces varnishes less coloured, " but less resistant, than the hard copal (copal-dur)."   (31.)

The temperatures at which these gums fuse are not very easy to arrive at; the statements made on this point are somewhat confusing, if not conflicting. This is, however, not surprising, for the determination of the fusing-point of substances of this kind is perplexing to most persons of moderate ability. These resins are very bad conductors of heat. Take an ounce of colophony (oxidized in a way which will be hereafter described), for instance, put it in a deep porcelain basin, heat the basin over a sand-bath. Soon the part of the resin in contact with the basin will fuse, a semi-fluid film will adhere to the surface of the basin. Now the lump of resin may be left at rest or turned and kneaded, but it will be found impossible to cause the parts of the resin not in actual contact with the basin to approximate, in temperature, to the parts which are directly heated.

When, therefore, 360° C. is given as the temperature necessary for the fusion of hard copal, 230° as that for soft copal (demi-dur), it is understood that these are the temperatures of the interior surface of the vessel containing the resin or of the gas or vapour within it. The temperature of a mass of several pounds of copal can never, even when fused, approach uniformity.

M. Naudin continues his description:—" The operator places in " a vase-shaped copper vessel, with a flat bottom, about 4 kilo- " grammes of hard copal. The copper vessel is then put over a " furnace with a brisk fire. The mass crepitates, water is given off " (N.B. the resin was previously carefully dried), " the resin fuses. " To prevent adhesion one stirs continually with an iron spatula. " The water having been driven off, pungent vapours of a ruddy " colour rise from the orifice of the vase. When all the resin is " fused, which one ascertains by testing the mass with the spatula, " 1,500 to 2,000 grammes of boiled linseed-oil, heated to 150° C., " are poured into the vase and its contents are well stirred to " favour solution." " Supposing all to have gone well this compound " of linseed-oil and copal is diluted with oil of turpentine at once, " while it is still hot, to bring it to the necessary state of fluidity " for a varnish."

But if too little oil of turpentine be added, if the varnish is too thick—and this defect is discovered after the varnish has cooled— it cannot then be further diluted; if cold oil of turpentine be added to the cool varnish, precipitation takes place, and the varnish is spoiled. In fact, it would appear that, after the varnish has once been completed and allowed to cool, there is no known method by which its fluidity may be increased by adding oil of turpentine, hot or cold.

This is the case only with hard copal made into a varnish in the way described; it would appear that a varnish made with soft copal, at a comparatively low temperature, may be diluted at pleasure.

The production of an oil-varnish from hard copal can be effected only in the way described. At first sight, it would appear to be a very strange proceeding to expose a quantity of resin or gum (which, as already explained, is a very bad conductor of heat) to the action of a brisk fire, in a copper vessel, until the temperature reaches 360° C., and then, when the resin fuses at this high temperature, to add linseed-oil at 150° C., in order to effect its solution. The fluid oil, by conduction and convection, conveys heat much better than the solid, bad-conducting resin can possibly do. Why not pulverize the resin, mix it intimately, in the desired proportions, with the oil and subject this intimate mixture to the necessary degree of heat to induce solution ? Or, more simple still, why not mix together the powdered resin, the linseed-oil and the oil of turpentine, in their relatively correct proportions to form a varnish, raising this mixture to 360° C. (if this temperature is really necessary) to promote solution ? All these plans have been tried and have been found to be unsuccessful.

M. Naudin describes the experiments which have been made in this direction:—1st. The proposal of M. P. Schützenberger in 1856 to effect combination of gum, oil, and essence in an autoclave at 300° C., duration 2 hours; 2nd. A new attempt of M. H. Violette in 1866 with the same object. Temperature 350-400°; pressure about 20 atmospheres.

The information which M. Naudin gives as to the chemistry of copal and the effects which heat produces on this substance is sufficient to explain the causes of failure, at least in a great measure. He writes (28):—" The most oxygenated resins are the most " soluble." " Filhol has demonstrated, besides, that if the hard, " half-hard, and soft copals shewed notable differences in their " physical properties, their centesimal composition was very nearly " the same."

As to the effects of heat (29):—" It is only by depolymerizing " it towards 360°, by naked fire, that one succeeds in overcoming " its insolubility. Liquid volatile products (isomers of essence of " turpentine C^{10} H^{16}) are thus obtained together with modified " copal (pyrocopal). But it must be distinctly said that this new " property is obtained only by changing the properties of the gum.

" Tingry acknowledged this by saying, ' The fire profoundly changes
" ' the copal, and leaves it neither the elasticity nor the tenacity
" ' which it possesses in its natural state.' "

" As early as 1860, Schiller had extracted an isomer of turpentine
" from copal. A similar fact had been observed by Dœpping with
" amber."

" More recently Schwarz has made an elementary analysis of
" pyrocopal; from which he concludes that the body resulting
" from the action of naked fire is richer in carbon and poorer in
" hydrogen and oxygen than the initial substance. In fact, one
" always finds a very considerable quantity of water in the crude
" oil of copal."

From this information it is not difficult to deduce some of the
reasons why the experiments to which reference has been made
have failed, and must always fail:—1st. In order to be soluble the
copal molecule must retain a certain amount of oxygen. 2nd. The
first effect of heat is the splitting of the molecule into a hydrocarbon
and an oxide. 3rd. If the heat continues, the oxide becomes
dehydrated; if dehydration is carried too far insolubility ensues.

The apparent object of the operator in the ordinary process is
to fuse the resin as rapidly as possible and to effect solution in the
oil before extensive dehydration has time to take place. The
temperature of the oil being only 150° C., its admixture rapidly
reduces that of the copper vessel and its contents; as soon as
possible after solution, dilution with oil of turpentine still further
reduces the temperature. These apparently necessary conditions
are not complied with in the autoclave.

The effect of 360° C. on the copal is evidently not fusion, pure
and simple; the ultimate product (the volatile hydrocarbon excepted)
is obviously a dehydrated oxide (a colophone).

But, apart from the causes of failure which have been suggested,
it must be observed that linseed-oil has an affinity for oxygen which
is somewhat greater than that of the terpenes (at any rate, when
little degraded from the hydrocarbons); further, it will hereafter
be demonstrated that when oil of turpentine is heated (even at
100° C.) with the other constituents of a varnish it also has a

tendency towards important changes of constitution.   Herein lies the probable explanation of the difficulties attending the further dilution of a varnish after it has been completed and cooled.

The effect, therefore, of heating together copal, linseed-oil and oil of turpentine to so great an extent as 300° C. and upwards, must be exceedingly complex, owing not only to the changes in the copal, but also to the reaction of the three substances on each other; with special reference to the oxygen which they contain and their varying affinity for it under the conditions to which the mixture is exposed.

In the experiments which have been made it has been kept steadily in view that a clear understanding of these phenomena is of paramount importance in the production of varnish of the highest quality.

CHAPTER 5

OIL-VARNISH FROM TURPENTINE DERIVATIVES AND ITS APPLICATION

THE simple observation of the dichröism of the old varnishes would have afforded little indication of their actual composition had not this been soon followed by an additional clue.

On the 14th June, 1900, the brilliant morning light which streamed through an eastern window fell upon a panel of pitch-pine, not only revealing dichröism, but vividly recalling the two distinctive colours of the red Neapolitan varnish which had been the object of scrutiny more than a month before.

It is deplorable how much one sees and how little one observes ! Every day, for many years, panels of pitch-pine had been round about me; their admirable colour and figure (constantly changing according to direction, intensity and quality of light) could not be ignored; but, until now, I had failed to observe in their ever-varying shades a striking resemblance to the infinite colour variety of the old varnishes. Some of these panels had been covered with varnishes of different qualities: exposed to light and air for many years, the constituents of the wood had become slowly oxidized; others had been oxidized by artificial means, devised to imitate these effects of time; in many cases, the results of these two processes, natural and artificial, are incapable of distinction.

The artificial process was very simple; it was varied in three ways:—1st. The finished wood was lightly coated with ordinary nitric acid; in a short time spontaneous oxidation ensued. 2nd. The nitric acid was diluted with an equal volume of water; after its application, heat was necessary to induce a reaction. 3rd. The surface of the wood was saturated (more or less) with linseed-oil previous to oxidation (the panel which resembled the Neapolitan varnish was known to have been so treated). In all cases, after the completion of the oxidation process, the panel was washed with water and, when perfectly dry, was polished with alcoholic solution of shellac (French polish).

The colours produced by these three variations of the oxidation process may be thus briefly described in general terms: those of the first and of the natural effects of time, transmission—yellow to yellow-brown; refraction—light red, deep orange, red-brown. Those of the second method are similar to those of the first, but tend more and more towards brown according to the degree and duration of the heat employed to induce the oxidation reaction. The colours of the third variety are deeper and more crude: the ground colour is yellow, buff, or orange; that of refraction is red (sometimes approaching crimson) and red-brown.

It will be evident that in attempting to describe these colours of the wood all the different characteristics of the old varnishes of Brescia, Cremona, Venice, Naples, &c., have been portrayed.

The term " pitch-pine " seems to have been originally used to designate the wood of pinus rigida; but the fine wood of commerce which bears this name to-day is doubtless mainly the produce of pinus palustris, with the occasional unwelcome intrusion of that of pinus tæda, a timber of vastly inferior quality.

The prevailing and characteristic property of this wood (as its name denotes) is its almost complete saturation with turpentine products. Pitch-pine is, in general, very elastic.

A few weeks' study and investigation demonstrated the fact (naturally surmised) that the dichröism and colour effects which have been described are due to the presence of terpenes in different stages of oxidation, more or less dehydrated.

Wherever the cradle of the violin may have been, it may be safely assumed that a bit of resin was in it, as surely as this substance is to be found in every fiddle-case to-day. The geographical position of Brescia indicates it as a most likely place in which to seek resin, as well as other products of conifers. It lies on the western shore of the Lago di Garda, whose opposite shore, especially towards the north, approaches the pine-clad hills of Austrian Tyrol.

The surroundings of Venice are widely different from those of Brescia; but, if we may judge from the fact that turpentine has been an article of commerce from that city from time immemorial, larch-trees must abound at no very great distance.

It is of interest to notice that although larch-wood is elastic, it is appreciably less so than is pitch-pine.

It has already been demonstrated by the researches of M. Mailand, the results of which have been quoted, that the substances which were most used in Italy in the sixteenth century for making varnish were derived from the coniferæ of their own country. In fact, Alexis (1550) suggests only two other substances as constituents of oil-varnish, viz., mastic and sandarac (what particular gum he designated by this name is problematical).

Instead, therefore, of the old assumption that the violin-makers procured some remarkable gum (at present unknown, always rather mystical) for the basis of their varnish, it will be assumed that they used substances which they certainly had near at hand, both cheap and abundant. It will further require no great stretch of the imagination to suppose that the Venetians had mainly at their disposal the products of larch (Larix Europæa), while the Brescians and Cremonese had greater abundance of those of the pines and fir-trees (Pinus, Abies, and Picea).

The turpentines most easily available to-day are resin and oil of turpentine from America, the produce of several varieties of pine, and Venice turpentine from larch. Ordinary commercial samples have been used in the experiments to be described; their origin is unfortunately but unavoidably unknown; their quality has been found to be good, invariably suited to the purpose for which they were procured.

Henceforth a distinction will be made which is purely arbitrary: varnishes derived from resin and oil of turpentine (which are looked upon as products of pinus) will be called Cremonese: while, on the other hand, those derived from Venice turpentine (a larch product) will be called Venetian. Neapolitan varnish might have as its terpene constituent either the one form or the other; the quality which characterizes it depends upon its mode of preparation, which will be hereafter explained.

The drying oil used will be assumed to be linseed-oil; this is the oil which the old authors on varnish appear to have known. Cremona, especially, appears to have gained a reputation for the excellent quality of its linen; flax must have grown in the adjacent country, as in other parts of Italy, under conditions perfectly suited to its successful cultivation.

The choice of an oxidant for the terpenes was a matter that required a good deal of consideration and some experiments. Not the slightest trace of any oxidant is to be found among the authors cited by M. Mailand, or elsewhere. It is conceivable that, at any rate in the earliest times, the old varnish-makers may have availed themselves of the well-known oxidizing powers of the essence; but if so, even with the advantage of the warmth and sunlight of Italy, it must have been a slow process indeed. Life is too short to think of it as an available oxidant in this temperate and comparatively sunless climate !

Nitric acid was finally selected, and has proved to be well adapted in every respect for the purpose. Whether the reduction of the nitrogen is complete or only partial, the gaseous and aqueous residues are readily and entirely eliminated by heat. Its precise mode of application was less easy to determine. The method employed for the production of terephthalic acid was rejected as too energetic and selective, besides being wasteful; that eventually adopted will sufficiently appear from the experiments now to be described.

If to 100 parts of oil of turpentine there be added about 50 parts of colophony or of Venice turpentine, the whole warmed and mixed, a fluid results of convenient consistency for heating in a glass, tubulated retort. With this viscous fluid, 3 to 5 parts of ordinary pure nitric acid (sp. gr. about 1·420), added drop by drop, are intimately mixed by stirring. On gently heating this mixture (over a water-bath) a reaction will begin, the violence of which may be moderated by removing the source of heat for a time. When effervescence abates, the retort may be again heated, for some hours, until the reaction is practically at an end. When cold, more nitric acid is added, the same process being repeated. This process of nitrification and oxidation is several times repeated; the resulting varnish is finally heated over the water-bath (at 100° C.) for many hours.

During the progress of this experiment the following phenomena may be observed. At first the nitric acid has a tendency to fall to the bottom of the retort, but by continued mixing the turpentine becomes turbid and of a brown colour. When the oxidation reaction begins, the turpentine soon passes to a yellow colour, which deepens as the oxidation proceeds; all turbidity disappears. Seen in bulk the fluid passes from orange to red; soon only red rays pass through it; at first, the red rays of a reading-lamp can easily permeate three inches; but as the experiment proceeds it becomes less and less translucent, although it is not turbid. After heating for several hours, when the nitric acid has been, apparently, long since all decomposed, bubbles of vapuor or gas continue to rise through the fluid. A little volatile oil distils over into the receiver, accompanied always by water having an acid reaction and an odour of acetic acid.

This volatile oil has a specific gravity of 0·861 at 18° C. Its boiling point is not constant, but is about 155° to 156°. It is optically inactive. (The oil of turpentine used had sp. gr. 0·869 at 17½° C. and was strongly dextro-rotatory.) This oil therefore resembles terebene, which has the same odour.

When cool, the varnish in the retort is strongly dichröic. It is decanted. At the bottom and near the sides of the retort a small quantity of red resin is found, which is insoluble in oil of turpentine, freely soluble in aqueous alcohol, also soluble in warm linseed-oil.

At the bottom of the retort there is a minute quantity of watery fluid; when this is mixed with a little absolute alcohol, crystals of an organic acid immediately separate; they possess the characteristics of succinic acid (as far as can be judged from so small a quantity).

The fluid decanted is a turpentine-varnish possessing the desired qualities of colour and dichröism. The red resin found in the retort clearly indicates that such a varnish has its limits as a solvent. The insolubility of this part of the oxidized terpene was found to arise from dehydration, caused by contact with the heated glass of the retort. From the fact that this red substance is readily soluble in linseed-oil, it may be inferred that the red varnishes were certainly oil-varnish.

Turpentine-varnish produced in this way, from either colophony

v.   4

or Venice turpentine, is of the highest quality, as far as transparency, colour, and brilliancy are concerned. It dries very slowly, but in a month or six weeks a pellicle of the usual thickness seems to become perfectly dry. If it is then rubbed briskly with the fingers, the surface pulverizes. If this powder is removed by a cloth or brush, the surface which remains (only a small part of the varnish has been removed) is dull and opaque; but in a few hours it regains its former brilliance and translucence. The cohesion destroyed by the friction of the skin is restored after a period of rest.

A thin pellicle of this same varnish applied to a door has borne ordinary wear for some years. It has been also found that thicker pellicles have slowly become quite solid. If such a varnish were made over a charcoal stove or similar directly-heating apparatus, it would precisely resemble the old varnishes of Brescia. The pellicle would be entirely soluble in alcohol, and therefore when dry could not be distinguished from that formed from a spirit varnish. This is a probable explanation of the statement by M. Fétis that Maggini's were spirit varnishes; a spirit varnish at the time of Maggini seems to be an anachronism.

After some few practical experiments with these simple turpentine-varnishes, it became evident that the best remedy for this want of cohesion was the addition of a certain proportion of linseed-oil (boiled). The old makers appear to have been led to the same conclusion. There are no indications as to the amount which they used; but, from the evidence of the varnishes, it is apparent that it was restricted to an approximate minimum. The formulæ of Watin and Martin, given by M. Naudin, have been useful guides; the results have proved satisfactory.

An oil-varnish cannot, however, be properly prepared by simply adding linseed-oil to a turpentine-varnish; it requires a special mode of manufacture, which will be now described. Firstly, what may be called the " dry way," will be given:—

Colophony (such as is used for common purposes, and is found in commerce as rosin) is pulverized, in a mortar of Wedgwood porcelain, with a pestle of the same material. To this fine powder is added 20 to 25 per cent. of nitric acid. The acid is added drop by drop (from a pipette), and is quickly kneaded and mixed with the colophony, by the pestle, so as to prevent, as far as possible, unequal action. If this operation is deftly performed, very little rise of temperature will take place; the result will be a rather dark, olive-green powder, somewhat granulated, which is quite stable at atmospheric temperatures. This nitro-colophone is, to this extent, a mild explosive: it requires a temperature approaching 100° C. to cause its decomposition; when this begins, heat is generated by the reaction, consequently, decomposition proceeds with constantly increasing speed as the temperature rises, until, if the quantity dealt with be large, a violent reaction will eventually ensue.

It is difficult for the gas and vapour evolved to escape from the viscuous mass, which, as soon as the reaction commences, swells and froths; it is necessary, on this account, to conduct the operation in a vessel (preferably a deep porcelain basin) of sufficient capacity to retain the frothing resin.

To excite the reaction the vessel containing the nitro-colophone may be heated over a water-bath, the temperature of which is quite sufficient for the purpose.

If an excess of nitric acid be allowed to remain in contact with a part of the colophony, a reaction will there commence and spread to the whole (without extraneous heating).

During the reaction the hot resin may be stirred, with a glass or porcelain rod or spatula, to facilitate the escape of steam, nitrogen and some of its lower oxides; the heat of the bath should be maintained for a sufficient time (half-an-hour to an hour) until the resin has been practically freed from these products of decomposition.

The colophony, thus oxidized by the reduction of the nitrogen, will be found to have undergone a complete change, chemical and physical. Its colour, if the proportion of nitric acid (effectively used) has been at least 25 per cent. of the colophony, will be a bright, pure yellow (very much resembling gamboge); if the proportion of nitric acid has been considerably less than 25 per cent., the colour of the product will be less pure, inclining to brown. Its fusing point will be raised above that of the original colophony.

Parenthetically, it may be here remarked that the fusing point

(135° C.) usually attributed to colophony appears to be considerably too high (the difficulty attending such determinations with these very bad conductors of heat has been already alluded to). If a little finely-pulverized colophony be shaken on to the surface of boiling water, the powder will rapidly melt into oily globules. If a quantity of this powder be placed, in the form of a cone, in a porcelain basin and be exposed to the temperature of a water-oven (about 97° C.), for a short time, it will fuse into a clear, homogeneous viscid substance having a horizontal surface and every other attribute of a fluid. In linseed-oil and in oil of turpentine colophony fuses at the temperature of the water-bath; consequently, the heat of this apparatus has been always found to be sufficient to aid its speedy solution in these menstrua. It seems, therefore, that the fusing-point of colophony cannot be above 100° C.

The mode of oxidation of colophony just described is not very convenient (except, perhaps, where the object in view is the production of spirit-varnish), because it is not always easy to ensure an even mixture of the nitric acid before oxidation begins; it may easily happen that a few drops of nitric acid may, inadvertently, have time to attack a small portion of the colophony, raising its temperature sufficiently to initiate a reaction, before general and uniform nitrification has taken place.

The subsequent steps in the formation of an oil-varnish from this oxy-colophone will sufficiently appear in the treatment of similar substances produced by the " wet way " of oxidizing, which is more convenient and effective, and which will now be described.

Colophony is dissolved in about half its weight of oil of turpentine, which is sufficient to form with it a viscid fluid, convenient for stirring. With this the necessary proportion of nitric acid is blended, the acid being cautiously added, in small quantities at a time (preferably from a dropping pipette or bottle), until, by continued stirring, an even mixture or compound is obtained. If during this operation the temperature should rise more than a few degrees, the containing vessel should be cooled by immersion in water.

Venice turpentine generally furnishes, in its usual viscous state, a suitable substance for the process just described; if a little too thick, it may be easily thinned by admixture of a little essence.

The nitrification of oil of turpentine is easily effected by this method.

The object of the operator should be to ensure complete nitrification before proceeding to decomposition. The progress of nitrification may be easily observed by the change of colour of the terpene, combination being always attended by deepening brown.

A little experience will show that the farther the terpene has been removed (by degradation) from the hydrocarbon the more rapidly it will be attacked by the nitric acid; nitro-colophone will be formed in a few hours, while nitro-pinene (from oil of turpentine) will need as many days. As a clear understanding of this matter is of importance, it will be necessary here to describe in detail the preparation of the latter substance.

A quantity of well-rectified, perfectly colourless, dextro-rotatory oil of turpentine (*d*-pinene) is placed in a deep porcelain basin (of a capacity largely exceeding the volume of the fluid); 10 per cent. (by volume) of pure nitric acid (sp. gr. 1·420) is added to it, drop by drop, well mixed by stirring with a spatula (glass or porcelain). Slight rise of temperature takes place, which may, if necessary, be controlled as already directed. The turbid mixture, on standing, divides into two strata: the upper (terpene) colourless; the lower (residue of nitric acid) red-brown. After standing for a few hours, a further 10 per cent. of nitric acid is added, as before; on dividing, the upper stratum remains, apparently, unchanged. After standing for two days, the upper stratum has become of a pale brown; the red-brown colour of the lower is fading. A further 10 per cent. of nitric acid is added precisely as before. Rise of temperature is now scarcely perceptible; on dividing, the upper layer has become of a deeper brown. The characteristic odour of oil of turpentine has disappeared and an odour of fir-wood is substituted. The mixture is allowed to stand for two more days; at the end of this time, the upper stratum has become of a dark-brown colour, the lower is almost colourless. Nitrification of the terpene is now supposed to be practically complete.

It will be obvious, from what has been described, that in the nitrification of a complex solution, such as one formed of colophony and oil of turpentine, or Venice turpentine alone (which is evidently a solution of isomerides and oxides in essential oil), the effect will be quite different whether a short or a long time is allowed for the process: the nitric anhydride will combine first of all with dehydrated oxides, later with oxides, and finally with the hydrocarbon itself. Nitrification may be confined to the action of a few hours, or may be extended to ten or twenty days, according to the intentions of the operator as to the constitution of the resinous part of his varnish.

It will be remembered that the pitch-pine panel, whose colours were observed to correspond with those of an old Neapolitan varnish, was known to have been saturated with linseed-oil previous to oxidation. It is easily surmised from this that the Neapolitan types were produced in this way: Some varnish-maker (here again I suspect the influence of some chemical student of the Church of Rome) observed that the transformation of raw drying-oil into the more siccative form is precisely on all-fours with the oxidation of turpentine. The old process was modified in accordance with this view.

The first stage in the preparation of a Neapolitan varnish is this: Colophony or Venice turpentine is dissolved in raw linseed-oil (by means of a water-bath) in proportions suitable for the constitution of an oil-varnish, say about two parts of terpene to one part of oil. This oleo-terpene is nitrified in precisely the same way as that already prescribed for the terpenes alone. The disadvantage of the Neapolitan method is that the affinities of the two substances (turpentine and oil), acted upon together, are not quite the same; consequently in the different stages of the preparation of the varnish, the transformations do not proceed pari passu (they tend rather in the opposite direction to that which is desired, as will be presently explained); in this case, nitrification should not be prolonged.

Having thus prepared nitro-terpene or nitro-oleo-terpene, the succeeding stage—oxidation, by the decomposition of the nitro-compound—may proceed.

The most convenient and safe method of performing this operation is to place over a boiling water-bath a capacious empty porcelain basin; to this transfer the nitro-compound in suitable successive portions until the whole has been decomposed. If it is desired to attempt this transformation in the same basin in which nitrification has been effected (which is practicable after a little experience), the best plan is to warm the basin on one side only, so as to initiate the reaction at a point near the surface of the mass; in this way, by a little management and care, decomposition may be gradually extended to the whole mass.

The oxidized resin or oelo-resin is allowed to remain over the water-bath until decomposition is quite complete and until the residual water of the nitric acid and its gaseous products have been driven off, this object being assisted by constant stirring; this may be generally attained in about an hour.

The oelo-resin (for Neapolitan varnish), while still hot, is diluted with oil of turpentine, as desired.

A requisite quantity of boiled linseed-oil is added to the oxy-terpene, in which it soon dissolves, the temperature of the bath being well maintained; the resulting thick varnish may be then diluted, by the gradual admixture of oil of turpentine, to any extent that may be desired.

All the varnishes thus produced are of a yellow colour, of varying depth: the colours of the Cremonese, Venetian, and Neapolitan varieties are somewhat different; by persons well acquainted with their distinguishing tints they may generally be identified without much difficulty. They are very transparent, perfectly bright and clear; owing to their powers of refraction and marked dichröism, they exhibit perfectly the grain and every fibre of the wood on which they are laid.

In the case of these varnishes, the addition of linseed-oil is not a necessity for the purpose of solution; for the resin, provided oxidation and subsequent heating have been confined within reasonable limits, is perfectly soluble in oil of turpentine; generally, no unusual precautions need be taken in diluting the varnish with that vehicle. Oil is added to the varnish to increase its cohesion and durability.

When the vehicle evaporates (after the application of the varnish) the pellicle is of a soft character. Wood, unless it is very dense, absorbs considerable quantities of these varnishes; consequently the pellicle is adhesive. Such varnishes harden very slowly; long after the surface has become so dry as to bear polishing, the varnish is sufficiently plastic to receive impressions when contact, accompanied by pressure, is long continued. Instruments covered with them require to be exposed to warm, dry air for many months before they are in a condition to bear handling and wear without injury. As may be supposed, the varnish remains perfectly elastic, and, as far as may be judged from the experience of some years, never loses that quality.

In every respect, therefore, these yellow varnishes, with refractions of orange and light-red, are eminently adapted for covering musical instruments. To those who have a taste for delicate colouring, their beauty cannot be surpassed; but for others who prefer colours which are more vivid or more sombre (who find a lurid, stormy sunset more entrancing than that of perfect summer weather) it is necessary to provide varnishes of a more rufous character. Their mode of production will be now described.

Having produced an oxy-terpene or resin in the way described, it is necessary to expose this substance to a carefully-regulated temperature at or above that of the water-bath, for certain specified times. The increased depth, as well as the particular shade, of colour will depend upon these factors—temperature and duration.

It has been already explained that these resinous substances are singularly bad conductors of heat. They are at the same time very viscid; conduction and convection are both wanting. To increase these attributes, it is convenient to add now to the oxy-terpene (which is supposed to remain in the basin in which it was formed) the quantity of pure siccative linseed-oil required for the constitution of the varnish: equal, generally, to from 30 to 50 per cent. of the weight of the initial colophony or Venice turpentine.

The porcelain basin is removed from the water-bath to a sand-bath (or any other apparatus by which a gentle heat may be communicated); the temperature is gradually raised above 100° C., while the contents of the basin are well stirred. In the course of an hour (if the rise of temperature has been slow) the colour of the varnish will be seen to be deepening; this change will be increased and intensified, according to the duration of time and the degree of temperature, until a deep chocolate brown will be reached. The varnish may now be diluted with oil of turpentine, but this operation requires to be performed with caution. It is preferable to warm the essence to a degree nearly approaching the temperature of the varnish; if this precaution is not taken, the cold essence must be incorporated (by stirring) very gradually, the temperature of the varnish being meantime well maintained.

If a still darker varnish is required, the heating may be continued for a longer time, or the temperature may be raised. The varnish, in bulk, will then after a certain time appear almost black; when seen in a thick film on the surface of the white basin or of the porcelain spatula, it will have a deep red tint; in a thin film the colour remains a shade of yellow. To dilute this dark varnish requires some practice and skill. If too much oil of turpentine be added, if too much be added at one time, if by dilution the varnish be cooled below a certain point (all factors incapable of exact definition), precipitation takes place, the varnish is spoiled. It must be made over again with new materials.

Varnishes which have been heated in this way, so as to be subjected, wholly or in part, to a temperature appreciably exceeding 100° C., have always a brown tint.

It will be expected that the implements and tools used by the earliest violin-makers of Brescia and Cremona were a little primitive; it is not to be supposed that a " balneum mariæ " was to be found among them, although there is little doubt that it was known in the middle of the sixteenth century. At first it may be supposed that varnishes were made in a pot over a charcoal brazier or some such crude heating apparatus; careless makers very likely reverted to this primitive apparatus long after the " balneum mariæ " had come into general use. To some method of direct heating the examples of brown varnish, so often seen on many of the older instruments, must, without any doubt, be attributed.

The uncertainty of result attending the use of the sand-bath, or any method of direct heating, soon induced me to abandon it in favour of the water-oven, whose temperature can be constantly maintained at about 97° C. (the water-bath has also been occasionally used). Although the process is rather tedious (lasting from three to seven hours), the results are good in every way. Varnishes made by this means have not often been found difficult to dilute at the completion of the process. The requisite quantity of oil of turpentine, in a suitable flask, can be introduced into the water-oven previous to its use, so that it may acquire the same temperature as the varnish before admixture.

Varnishes of pure shades of orange and red may be thus produced.

Whatever the source of heat employed, it may be observed that when the solution (of oxy-terpene in linseed-oil) has been heated for some time at about 100° C. or upwards, it begins again to froth; when stirred, bubbles of vapour rise through it. This vapour is steam. In every process employed it has been found that when an oxy-terpene is heated, as the colour deepens, minute quantities of water are given off. This water is not attributed to the residue of the nitric acid, but to chemical change in the terpene oxide, which becomes dehydrated (H_2O is eliminated).

As a consequence of this dehydration, the terpene molecule becomes (centesimally) more rich in carbon, losing two atoms of hydrogen and one of oxygen; the varnish, of which the resin is so important a constituent, becomes slightly less transparent; its apparent colour passes from yellow to orange, red or brown; its other physical properties change also—it is less soluble in oil of turpentine, its viscosity is greater; when the pellicle of varnish is eventually formed it appears to solidify more quickly, and is of a somewhat harder quality than that formed from the oxy-terpenes.

If the information given by M. Naudin (already quoted) is carefully considered, it will be evident that in the preparation of copal varnish the phenomena are identical with those which have been described. Pyrocopal is evidently a dehydrated oxy-terpene derived from copal. It appears that the qualities attributed to varnishes derived from copals of different degrees of hardness are quite as likely to be due to the different temperatures to which the copals are subjected as to any material difference in the primary substances themselves.

It will now be understood what an immense variety of varnishes, differing in apparent colour and in other respects, can be produced from the same original materials by modifications of the two factors of oxidation and dehydration. The proportion of nitric acid may be increased from 10 per cent. to 30 per cent. and upwards; the time allowed for nitrification may be a few hours or many days; the extent of dehydration (which is obviously dependent in a great measure on that of oxidation) is limited only by the question of solubility: excess of oxidation and dehydration means absolute insolubility as far as an oil-varnish is concerned. In general terms, the progress of degradation (oxidation and dehydration) of a terpene hydrocarbon is marked by gradual decrease of solubility in oil of turpentine and linseed-oil and a similar increase of solubility in aqueous alcohol.

In consequence of this it will be found that while with an oxy-terpene 30 per cent. of linseed-oil is quite sufficient to constitute a good varnish, 50 per cent. will be absolutely required for solution as dehydration extends, with a still further increase as degradation proceeds.

Given imperfect methods of determining the proportion of oxidant to terpene (no very easy matter where a fluid is concerned, for even now the part capable of conversion to a resin can be only roughly estimated), a charcoal stove or some equally crude mode of heating, it would be practically impossible to produce two varnishes precisely alike.

Another variable factor in the production of an oil-varnish is the proportion of oil, which influences not the colour only, but other physical properties as well. As to oxidation and dehydration, the desired colour of the varnish is some guide, experience enables the operator to produce a close approximation to a given varnish; but with respect to the proportion of oil to resin, so far no rule has been found. Practical copal-varnish makers appear to test a drop of the solution of oil and resin, cooled on a plate of glass, judging by its character as to the sufficiency of the oil. With a hard resin this may be practicable, but, with one that is comparatively soft, no reliable indication is apparent.

The quality of a varnish, apart from its colour and brilliancy, can be judged only after it has become hard enough to be finished and polished. Under ordinary circumstances, in this climate, this is a question of at least six months. Experience must be the outcome of many years.

The boiled linseed-oil of commerce, even the better qualities used for artistic purposes, will be seldom found of sufficient purity for fine varnish. In the early stages of these experiments, great difficulty was experienced in obtaining a supply of siccative oil free from mineral impurity. It is more than probable that the existence of equal difficulty in the olden times led eventually to the invention of the Neapolitan method, in which raw linseed-oil may be directly used. But in avoiding Scylla the old varnish-makers ran great risk of falling into Charybdis, as a little consideration will show.

The main object of the introduction of oil into a varnish is to increase its cohesion and toughness. The extent of the oxidation of a drying-oil to render it suitable for this purpose is small: from 5 to 10 per cent. of nitric acid would be amply sufficient. If oxidation is carried much further than this the oil becomes resinous, its essential attribute is destroyed. Neapolitan varnishes have been made (in the course of these experiments) which, when dry, pulverized by friction precisely in the same way as turpentine-varnishes (without oil). No doubt many such varnishes were made and used in the olden time; as a consequence, some modern experts have designated them as spirit-varnishes, in the same way as Fétis so described the varnishes of Maggini.

The Neapolitan varnish-maker was consequently on the horns of a dilemma: on the one hand he was restrained by the consideration that oxidation beyond a certain point destroys the most valuable property of his oil (as far as an oil-varnish is concerned); while, on the other hand, the showy red varnish, which he often desired, could only be reached through oxidation far beyond this point. The oil was required to play a dual rôle, which required the development of two totally different attributes.

The manufacture of yellow varnish was easy enough, for in this case a solution of colophony or Venice turpentine in raw linseed-oil could be nitrified and oxidized with a proportion of nitric acid compatible with the retention of the usual properties of a drying oil (say from 5 to 15 per cent. of the combined weight of the terpene and linseed-oil). Such varnish is often of excellent quality, and, if well made, not essentially different from a Cremonese or Venetian varnish made in the usual way—always understood that the oxidation of the oil is apt to be as much in excess as that of the terpene is too little. The pale varnishes of Alessandro Gagliano, of Naples, are examples of this class; M. Vidal writes of his instruments:—" His workmanship is careful and skilful; his " varnish only leaves something to be desired, notably in its " nuance of a yellow greyish tone (jaune fond grisâtre), little " pleasing to the eye." The oxidation of the terpenes is manifestly too little.

But for a red varnish, the transformation of part of the oil to a red-brown resin and the retention of the remainder in the form of a boiled oil are obviously incompatible with simultaneous treatment. The best mode of compromising this difficulty appears to be either: 1st. To add to the terpenes (colophony and/or Venice turpentine) a small amount of linseed-oil (raw), say about 10 per cent. of their weight; this oleo-terpene is diluted with oil of turpentine to a convenient consistency, nitrified with 25 or 30 per cent. of nitric acid, decomposed, dehydrated in a water-oven to the required depth of colour (4 to 6 hours); the resulting oleo-resin is dissolved in boiled linseed-oil (produced either in the ordinary way or by the oxidation of raw oil with a small proportion, such as 5 per cent., of nitric acid), as though it were a simple terpene resin, finally diluted with oil of turpentine as customary. Or, 2nd. In nitrifying the oleo-terpene as just described, about 5 per cent. less of nitric acid is used; after decomposition and dehydration, the oleo-resin is dissolved in raw linseed-oil and a further oxidation of the varnish, with $2\frac{1}{2}$ or 5 per cent. of nitric acid, is effected, again followed by dilution like an ordinary varnish. Of these two alternatives, in my hands, the first has given the most satisfactory results. Tononi, of Bologna, has left excellent examples of varnish of this kind.

It is somewhat difficult to imagine violin-makers like Gagliano and Tononi grappling with problems of this sort; here again the assistance of some student of chemistry appears probable.

As may be supposed, pale Neapolitan varnishes are perfectly transparent; the decrease of this quality in the red varnishes of this type is very apparent on the tables of the instruments which they cover; the backs and ribs are effective—there the slight want of transparency does not attract attention.

There is no difference whatever in the preparation of a varnish whether the initial ingredient is colophony, Venice turpentine, or oil of turpentine. The whole of the colophony will, however, remain in the varnish, whereas in the other cases an unknown quantity, being volatile and incapable of conversion to a resin, will be sooner or later evaporated and lost. In estimating the proportions of oxidant and oil, about 80 parts of colophony have been looked upon as equivalent to 100 parts of Venice turpentine and to about 160 parts of oil of turpentine.

Colophony and Venice turpentine do not produce varnishes of quite the same colour or quality, whether they are used in making Cremonese or Venetian varnish, or form part of a Neapolitan varnish. The larch product produces a varnish which is slightly, but appreciably, more pure in colour and more resistant than that which contains colophony. As far as experience goes, an instrument treated with Venetian varnish gives a tone which is more brilliant than that resulting from the softer Cremonese—as might be expected from the superior elasticity of pine wood as compared with that of larch.

Tone results lying between those attributed to these two types of varnish can be produced by blending Venice turpentine either with colophony or with oil of turpentine (in the latter case the nitrification process is prolonged); such mixtures of natural terpenes give rise to colours of a warmer tint than is obtainable by the use of either colophony or Venice turpentine alone.

*   *   *   *   *   *

On reading the descriptions of the old varnishes by various writers, it is significant that, while comparatively pale varnishes are, without exception, described as lightly and evenly laid on, those of a deeper tone are very often represented as having been thickly applied, crusted, used with want of care and skill, or as being more or less clotted (that these descriptions are true I can myself affirm). If the varnishes had been formed (as surmised) from a common basis, coloured to suit the taste of individual violin-makers, it would not be easy to explain this general agreement of description. He must be a clumsy operator indeed that cannot succeed in producing, from a given uniform basis varnish, coloured varieties approximating in qualities affecting their application.

When, however, we turn from these coloured concoctions to the pure oil-varnishes, whose mode of preparation has been described, an explanation is at once apparent: it must be looked for, not in the want of care or skill on the part of the artisan, but in the inherent properties of the varnish itself. A yellow varnish, whose basis is an oxy-terpene, is limpid, (with a little practice) easy of even application by means of a brush; but when this same varnish is heated for a few hours over a water-bath or in a water-oven, or for a much shorter time over a sand-bath, it becomes viscous, requiring a great deal of skill with the brush to lay on passably well. Neither can this deep-coloured, dehydrated varnish be diluted with oil of turpentine sufficiently to remove this practical inconvenience. It can be done by a large increase of oil, but then the effect of such a proceeding on the tone of the instrument, as well as on the brilliancy and colour of the varnish, must be considered. My opinion is that the old makers were quite right in rejecting this remedy; there is no room for doubt that those who take the trouble to study the question will unanimously endorse the conclusion at which I have arrived without any hesitation.

That there should be no possibility of doubt on this important question, the same varnish was made several times (involving a large expenditure of time and labour), in order to determine with exactness the minimum proportion of oil and limit of dilution with oil of turpentine consistent with its constitution. The details of this experiment will now be given, since the information which it affords and the light which it throws on the proceedings of the old makers are both instructive and interesting.

One hundred parts (1,200 grains or 80 grammes) of colophony were dissolved in 50 parts of oil of turpentine; this viscid fluid was nitrified with 33 parts of nitric acid (1·420), the nitrification being slow and extending over five or six days. The nitro-terpene was a dark-brown, plastic substance, almost solid; it could not be stirred with a porcelain spatula, but was cut out of the deep porcelain basin (6¼ inches or 16 centimetres diameter) in which it was prepared, with a knife, in suitable pieces for decomposition in a similar basin.

Decomposition was effected over a water-bath in the usual way. After the reaction, the resin was heated in a water-oven (with frequent stirring to facilitate the elimination of the aqueous residue of the nitric acid) for about an hour. Result—a yellow resin of a brilliant orange colour when seen in bulk. Dissolved over the water-bath, in 50 parts of linseed-oil (boiled), then diluted with 150 parts of oil of turpentine. The same varnish was made again and diluted with 180 parts of oil of turpentine. Both these varnishes were brilliant pale varnishes of a pure primrose-yellow colour when thinly spread on a white surface; a drop was copper-coloured. The red rays from a reading-lamp could easily pass through a thickness (in a flask) of about 3 inches diameter.

The oxy-terpene was made again (under identical conditions), but the resin was exposed to the heat of a water-oven (about 97° C.) for six hours (instead of one hour); it then became of a deep red colour when seen in bulk. It was dissolved in 50 parts of boiled linseed-oil and (being very thick and viscous) it was diluted with 250 parts of oil of turpentine. Hot, the varnish appeared to be good, but on cooling it became turbid; precipitation was so great that the varnish was useless.

The varnish was repeated again, the proportion of linseed-oil was increased to 55 parts, the oil of turpentine reduced to 180 parts. Precipitation, on cooling, was again considerable; after subsiding for a day or two, the decanted varnish was bright and fairly good.

Again the varnish was made—the linseed-oil increased to 60 parts, oil of turpentine diminished to 150 parts. The result was a perfectly bright, clear varnish, which required neither to be decanted nor filtered.

A thin film of this varnish is still yellow, but as the film thickens the colour deepens to a deep orange-red. A drop is the colour of a ruby. It is much less translucent than the first varnishes: the rays of the reading-lamp can no longer pass through a flask of it, although it has not the faintest trace of turbidity.

The viscosity of this varnish is very much greater than that of the first-made yellow varnishes; the latter are perfect varnishes for facility of application, but the former is difficult to lay on evenly without clots.

The 250 parts of oil of turpentine which were originally designed for this varnish would not have been too much to bring it to the same thickness as the yellow varnishes; but, as was clearly proved, even 180 parts were incompatible with the constitution of the varnish, with the assistance of an increase of 5 parts in the oil.

Were the resin heated still longer in the water-oven, it would become still more viscous and still less soluble in both linseed oil and in oil of turpentine. Dissolved in the same proportion of linseed-oil (60 parts), the dilution with oil of turpentine would have to be diminished, increase being manifestly impossible; the varnish would be of a deeper colour, but the difficulties of application would be augmented.

In the case of these deep-coloured varnishes, made from dehydrated oxy-terpenes, the conditions with which the operator has to contend are precisely similar to those attending the production of varnish from hard copal. It requires both experience and judgment to rightly determine the proper proportions of oil and essence. After the varnish has been completed and cooled, if it is too thin or too thick there is no known remedy; it cannot be heated again with a view to evaporation or dilution; if any attempt (ever so carefully performed) be made in this direction, the varnish will become turbid on cooling and will be spoiled. If, however, a varnish has been made which, on cooling, is found to be too thick or too thin, another similar varnish can be made with an equal tendency in the opposite direction; when quite cool, these two varnishes may generally be mixed in all proportions.

With all the varnishes, one element which militates against their perfectly even application is their absorption by the wood; if this absorption were uniform it could not affect the question, but its extent varies with the grain as well as the direction of the section of the wood. Naturally, when the section is parallel to the longer axes of the cylindrical fibres, the absorption of varnish is far less than when it is at an angle to these axes. Owing to the moulded shape of the back and table of violins, as well as to the variations

v. 5

in the grain of the wood, the angle of section is never constant. With every coat of varnish, therefore, especially the earlier coats, uneven absorption occurs, of necessity producing to some extent an uneven surface. Whether this was remedied by the old makers by " rubbing down " before the last coats were put on, or whether the varnishing was completed and then rubbed down and polished, can only be surmised: probably individuals had different methods in this respect.

No mode of reducing the finished varnish to a good and true surface has been found to equal rubbing down with a rubber kept well moïstened with alcohol of 87 to 90 per cent. Anyone who is expert at French polishing can perform this operation with perfect success without removing the smallest fraction of the varnish. It would be interesting to know whether Stradivari knew of this process.

Reference has already been made to the suggestion of M. Mailand that in order to prevent absorption of the varnish by the wood, it should be previously sized. This suggestion appears to arise from a total misconception of the whole varnish question; it needs no further discussion.

The various colours of the varnishes depend not on their actual colour (that which is seen when they are spread in a thin film on a smooth, white surface), but on that which is apparent when the thickness of the pellicle is sufficiently increased to allow of complicated refraction and reflection from varying planes. If their colour were a substantive one (the simple absorption of rays situated in one part of the spectrum and the reflection of the complement), such as that of a pigment, the different varnishes would cause little variety; the tone would be always yellow, tending more or less towards brown.

It will therefore be understood that the effect produced will mainly depend upon the quality of the varnish, the thickness of the film, and lastly, not least, the character of the wood on which it is laid.

When a new varnish is made it may be tested by application to a strip of maple or other wood; the result is some guide as to the probable appearance of a violin when covered with it, but to a very limited extent. Two backs of maple wood (both of fine figure and quality, but differing in the angle of section or in the original character of the wood) may be treated with the same varnish under precisely identical conditions; when finished it is difficult to believe that the varnish on the two instruments can be the same, so different is their apparent colour and general effect.

Apart, therefore, from the great variety in the characters of the varnishes, the additional factors of thickness of pellicle and of variation in the section or nature of the wood add to the complexity of the final results. It seems to be quite impossible to predict, with any precision, what will be the effect of the application of a known varnish to a virgin instrument.

There can be no doubt that some of the old violin-makers used repeatedly wood from the same log or tree; in this way the wood factor would be nearly a constant (not entirely so, for in the same tree adjoining sections will vary to a considerable extent). Keeping this one factor of wood an approximate constant, they may have striven, by change of varnish, towards their ideal of perfection. It is not at all difficult to understand that this pursuit of an ideal was fascinating; while the uncertain and surprising variety of results precluded their occupation from becoming monotonous.

In an Appendix will be given the details of a number of varnishes which have been prepared and used for musical instruments as well as for other purposes.

CHAPTER 6

INTERESTING CHEMICAL PROBLEMS WHICH HAVE PRESENTED THEM-
SELVES DURING THE PROGRESS OF THIS RESEARCH

THE earliest observation of dichröism in terpene products which has come under my notice is that of M. Berthelot, in 1853. It is to be regretted that he paid (or seemed to pay) no attention to it; at any rate, he unfortunately did not suggest any explanation of the phenomenon, which is to be understood in this restricted sense, that whereas the colour of transmission is yellow, that of refraction is red. Only once divergence from this general rule has been observed —an alcoholic solution of terpene derivatives from the bark of picea was seen to be yellow in a thin film, while in bulk the colour was purple. Neither, as far as I know, is any explanation to be found elsewhere, which is the more extraordinary, as it seems to be characteristic of a certain class of organic substances and its true significance cannot be without importance.

A striking instance of its occurrence is to be seen in the following experiment:—If oil of turpentine (d pinene), well rectified and colourless (sp. gr. 0·869; (a) $j = + 62·5$ at 18° C.), is mixed with aqueous alcohol (sp. gr. 0·830 at 18°), about five parts alcohol dissolve one part of pinene (by volume). To this alcoholic solution 5 per cent. of nitric acid (1·420) is added; a large globule of oil precipitates. The next day a further 5 per cent. of nitric acid is added, more oil separates; the whole of the separated oil (which amounts in volume to about one-fourth of that originally in solution) now rises to the surface. Shaken together at intervals, in four days the oil completely re-dissolves, solution again becomes perfect, all turbidity disappears. On the fifth day a further 5 per cent. of nitric acid is added, the same on the sixth day, without causing any change or turbidity (the alcohol-pinene solution now contains 20 per cent. of its volume of nitric acid). The solution slowly approaches a pale brown colour. In ten days, from the first addition of nitric acid, the colour has become distinctly yellow-brown (sherry), without any sign of dichröism. After standing for a month, in diffused daylight at about 16° C., the solution has become strongly dichröic, appearing in bulk of a deep red colour; it resembles a solution of oxidized colophony standing beside it, but is the darker of the two. A considerable amount of nitrous ether has been formed, the yellow-brown colour evidently denoted oxidation, pure and simple, of the pinene. My interpretation of the dichröism is that, with increased oxidation, the pinene has split; the solution now contains two terpenes having different optical properties: the red colour is due to interference.

The flask containing this solution is closed by a caoutchouc cork provided with a small glass tube drawn to a capillary point. Curiously enough, quite contrary to my expectations, this flask and its contents gradually—slightly but appreciably—increases in weight. After standing for several months, in strong diffused light, the colours are unchanged.

Another experiment:—10 grammes of colophony are slowly dissolved (at about 16°) in 10 c.c. of alcohol (0·830), one part of the former is therefore soluble in one of the latter at 16°. To this solution is added 5 c.c. of 20 per cent. nitric alcohol (1 to 4); turbidity immediately ensues; in half-an-hour the solution divides into two (about equal) strata, the upper more pale than the lower. These two strata are frequently well shaken and mixed together at intervals. The next day a mass of nodular crystals have separated (? sylvic acid). The crystals are filtered from the fluid, which is of a yellow-brown colour, strongly dichröic (it evidently still contains some of the crystallizable substance in solution). The crystals are much less soluble in the alcohol than the initial colophony, at least five times less; their solution is "sherry" coloured, not dichröic. When further oxidized by nitric alcohol, in a month it becomes (in diffused light) slightly dichröic, a thin film is pale yellow tinged with brown. This flask and its contents, closed also with a caoutchouc cork and capillary-pointed tube, slowly gains weight. The solution from which the crystals were separated, also further oxidized in the same way in a precisely similar flask, slowly loses weight.

The preparation of nitro-pinene (dextro oil of turpentine plus

30 per cent. of nitric acid) has already been described in detail. To effect decomposition, the brown fluid, separated from the aqueous residue of the nitric acid, is placed in a capacious porcelain basin over a boiling water-bath. As soon as the temperature of the nitro-pinene, in contact with the surface of the basin, approaches that of boiling-water, a reaction commences at the margin and soon extends, fumes of the lower oxides of nitrogen are thrown off, accompanied by steam; the reaction becomes general and rather violent, petty explosions eject small particles from the contents of the basin (these explosions are doubtless due to steam, produced by the heat of the reaction, which is prevented from escaping freely by the terpene). When the reaction is complete, the unpromising dull brown fluid has become converted into a brilliant yellow varnish, which, in bulk, appears of a rosy red colour. From this hot varnish clouds of vapour are escaping. The odour has again changed from that of fir- or pine-wood to a pleasant aromatic one. All water has entirely disappeared; the contents of the basin, on cooling, are found to be perfectly homogeneous, bright, clear, free from turbidity. This viscid, oily varnish is very slightly soluble in the oil of turpentine from which it was derived, when cold; warmed with it, it dissolves completely, but the bulk of the resin is precipitated on cooling. The varnish consists of a yellow resin (rosy red by refraction), dissolved in a volatile oil.

No varnish that has been made has had an odour, when cool, of oil of turpentine. The odour of this substance is so characteristic that it is difficult to believe that it could escape detection even though accompanied by aromatic substances. The volatile oil which takes its place appears to agree closely with it as to boiling point (about 155° to 156°, but not constant); specific gravity, 0·861; optically inactive. This agrees with terebene, with which its ethereal, faintly aromatic odour also corresponds. As may be understood, I had seldom opportunities for examining this volatile oil, but when I did so I found it invariably free from optical activity; this circumstance caused me some surprise, it appeared to me possible that, in some way, its activity had been destroyed; an attempt was made to determine this question. As the experiment is deemed to be of some importance, its details must be given.

Into a capacious tubulated glass retort were poured 100 c.c. of well-rectified oil of turpentine (supposed to be American) which was perfectly limpid and colourless. Its sp. gr. at $17\frac{1}{2}°$ was 0·869. In a 254 m.m. tube it gave for the transition tint, at $20° + 138°$ (my thirty years old Dubosc instrument and my old-fashioned methods will be excused).

With these 100 c.c. of pinene were carefully mixed, drop by drop, 5 c.c. of nitric acid. At intervals, during four days, the oil and the residue of the nitric acid were thoroughly mixed together. On the fifth day, the nitro-pinene was of a golden yellow colour, the residue of the nitric acid of a similar colour, a shade darker; the latter was now withdrawn by means of a pipette, some fragments of glass were introduced into the retort and it was placed over the water-bath.

When the water in the bath began to boil, bubbles of nitrogen, without colour or odour, rose through the fluid; the nitric acid was, apparently, completely reduced. When the temperature of the fluid reached 85° the reaction was fairly brisk; the evolution of gas reached its maximum at about 100° C. On signs of subsidence of reaction a sand-bath was substituted for the water-bath. At this stage the oxy-pinene was of a clear amber-yellow colour, no indication of dichröism. With the sand-bath (a gentle heat being applied) the temperature soon rose to 105°, at which a certain amount of reaction was still apparent; at 110° the evolution of gas practically ceased. At this temperature the colour of the liquid (hitherto constant) suddenly changed to a fine rosy red (dichröism); soon after it became turbid, then brown, finally (during the advanced stages of distillation) almost black.

At 145° the terpene began to boil (both oil and water condensed); it boiled briskly at 150°; temperature gradually rose to 153°, the liquid boiling very briskly. The oil now coming over had a pale green fluorescence. Dilute aqueous sodic carbonate (cold) dissolved from this a little oil of a yellow colour. The oil was well washed with distilled water, then dried with pure calcium chloride, when it was quite colourless:—sp. gr. 0·863 at 19°; rotation in 254 m.m. tube at 18°—64°. The fluid part of the contents of the retort was now poured into another retort; the solid part was left behind.

On resuming distillation, temperature rose to 158°; the distillate, washed and dried as before, was not quite colourless (not so easy to read in the polarimeter):—sp. gr. 0·860 at 19°; rotation in 254 m.m. tube at 18°—67/68°.

The first part of the distillate contained perhaps a little dextro-terpene.

Ignoring temperature, we get (for the formula (a) $j = \dfrac{100a}{\text{L.d}}$) for the original pinene (a) $j = +62\cdot5°$; for the distilled derivative (the mean of °67/68°) (a) $j = -30\cdot9°$.

The rotation of the inverted terpene approaches very closely to one-half of that of the original fluid.

Except that it was lævo-gyrose, this volatile oil could not be distinguished from that which I have always looked upon as terebene.

The dark brown substance remaining in the retorts was not a resin, but a soft aromatic substance. If, however, oxidation is carried further, as has been shown with 30 per cent. of nitric acid, pinene is partially converted into a resin of fine quality. So far, my efforts to obtain a resin from the volatile oil (or terebene), which is the other product of the oxidation of pinene, have not been successful.

Professor William Allen Miller gives a definite theory of the formation of resins (Organic Chemistry, 1869). He writes (625): " In the majority of cases the resins are formed by the oxidation " of the essential oils contained in the trees that yield them; hence " it is not surprising that in many instances they have the composition " of oxides of the hydrocarbon C20 H32, or of a hydrocarbon " derived from this, which has lost a certain number of atoms " of hydrogen in exchange for half that number of atoms of " oxygen." My efforts to discover a more modern theory, expressed in definite terms, have not been successful.

If oil,of turpentine (*d* pinene) may be taken as the type of the essential oils, it is certain that it may be oxidized (without other apparent change), by means of nitric acid, in the way described. Whether polymerisation accompanies this oxidation I do not know; perhaps it does. If oxy-pinene is subjected to heat it appears to split; the homogeneous fluid exhibits dichröism, quickly followed by turbidity. If oxidation has been considerable, and if the heat does not exceed 100° C., only dichröism is observed—solution remains perfect. A volatile hydrocarbon is evaporated or distilled, which under different conditions may be either optically inactive or lævo-gyrose. This hydrocarbon resembles the original pinene in density and boiling-point, but is quite different from it in its behaviour with nitric acid and its affinity for oxygen, which is far less. After many experiments and observations, the conclusion arrived at is that, let oxidation be much or little, drastic or very gentle, only a part of the terpene hydrocarbon is capable of conversion into a resin or resins. If this important fact should be confirmed by future investigators, the very interesting question must arise as to what happens, in Nature, to the other part of the hydrocarbon which is not transformed into a resin.

With respect to the oxide or resin, it may be dehydrated at 100° without decomposition or without becoming insoluble in its accompanying hydrocarbon; it may then be oxidized again, and again dehydrated. The limit of repetition of this double process of degradation has not been reached; difficulties of manipulation arise which, for an amateur, are not easy to deal with.

It does not appear, by any means, that dehydration is a necessary result of oxidation: its extent is determined by conditions which promote the elimination of water. It is essential for dehydration, however, that there shall be sufficient oxygen available—1st, to combine with two atoms of hydrogen; 2nd, to saturate an atom of carbon from which two atoms of hydrogen are detached; in consequence, two atoms of oxygen are necessary for every two atoms of hydrogen lost by the hydrocarbon. Experiments have shown that the extent of oxidation influences that of the succeeding dehydration.

The effect on solubility of this degradation of the hydrocarbon is not difficult to follow: increase of degradation causes decrease of solubility, firstly in oil of turpentine, secondly in linseed-oil; as solubility in these two menstrua decreases so does it steadily increase in aqueous alcohol. Affinity for oxygen increases as degradation proceeds.

Temperature not exceeding 100° appears to have no effect on an oxide or a resin beyond dehydration, but when higher temperatures are resorted to very complicated effects of decomposition enBue. These phenomena have been carefully studied and are well described by Rabaté and others. The brown colours produced whenever a sand-bath or other mode of direct heating is used are obviously due to one or more of these decompositions.

*   *   *   *   *   *

It has been surmised that with respect to varnish (or to a plastic resin) drying and solidification are not the same thing; for I have observed that all the varnishes continue slowly to solidify or harden for years after the laying on has been completed, while I am aware that, under the favourable conditions to which they are exposed (fairly dry air of a uniform temperature of about 16°), they must cease to lose weight by evaporation in a comparatively short time. It is impossible to demonstrate this with a violin because, as has been already shown, its own weight is never constant. A method of demonstration was arranged which is not open to this or, apparently, to any other objection.

Four slips of polished plate-glass (3 inches × 1) were, on one side, each coated with a different varnish. The surface of the glass was carefully cleaned, the varnish was poured on to it, the excess being drained off at one corner. The exact weight of each glass plate was known, they were subsequently weighed at specified times. The composition of the four varnishes was as follows:—

	No. 1.	No. 2.	No. 3.	No. 4.
Colophony	23·80	25·64		
Venice turpentine	...	...	25·50	36·60
Oil of turpentine (as solvent) ...	16·60	18·00	25·50	
Linseed-oil	11·90	15·36	12·24	12·20
Oil of turpentine (as diluent) ...	47·70	41·00	36·76	51·20
	100·00	100·00	100·00	100·00

The oil of turpentine used as solvent was employed to dissolve and thin the colophony or Venice turpentine previous to oxidation; a considerable part of it may therefore be expected to have been oxidized, a further unknown quantity evaporated in the subsequent processes. The oil of turpentine used as diluent was stirred into the varnish at the last stage of its preparation; as this operation was performed as expeditiously as possible (at a temperature below 100°) and as the varnish, when complete, was immediately, in all cases, transferred from the basin to a glass flask, then corked, the loss of this oil of turpentine cannot have been large.

No. 1, after oxidation, was heated in a water-oven about 1 hour.
No. 2, ,, ,, ,, ,, ,, ,, 6 hours.
No. 3, ,, ,, ,, ,, ,, ,, 6 ,,
No. 4, ,, ,, ,, ,, ,, ,, 7 ,,

On the 14th February, 1903, all the varnishes ceased to be adhesive, but they were all still comparatively soft. During the progress of the experiment there was no visible change of any kind in either of the varnishes.

The increase of weight after the minimum has been reached doubtless denotes absorption of oxygen from the air (comparatively dry, with a constant temperature of about 25°); under the circumstances, hydration is highly improbable.

It seems to be perfectly clear that part of the oil of turpentine, used as diluent, is permanently retained and forms part of the dry pellicle; this appears to be beyond all doubt. If the increase of weight, after the minimum, is rightly attributed to absorption of oxygen, this seems, from the relative proportions, to be referable to such part of the oil of turpentine and not to the linseed-oil.

This experiment clearly proves what has been surmised from numbers of less exact experiments—that solidification of a varnish or of a resin is generally quite a different thing from drying (evaporation of the volatile part of the pellicle); oxidation appears to play some part in the question, but it may be that, in the main, solidification denotes a gradual modification of physical form, perhaps polymerism.

If it is supposed that oxidation goes on after the evaporation has ceased, it must be equally assumed that a certain amount of oxygen is absorbed during the continuance of evaporation. In this case the figures recorded for the loss by evaporation must be

		WEIGHT.							
		Glass and Varnish.				Varnish.			
		No. 1.	No. 2.	No. 3.	No. 4.	No. 1.	No. 2.	No. 3.	No. 4.
Weight of glass ...		94·70	126·76	133·38	101·46	...	...	...	...
Date. 1902	Temp. C°								
3 Nov. ...	C°	98·80	133·48	136·70	111·23	4·10	6·72	3·32	9·77
4 ,, ...	23°	97·60	132·52	136·10	110·00	2·90	5·76	2·72	8·54
5 ,, ...	25°	97·50	132·33	136·00	109·70	2·80	5·57	2·62	8·24
6 ,, ...	23°	97·46	132·235	135·97	109·56	2·76	5·475	2·59	8·10
7 ,, ...	24°	97·43	132·17	135·94	109·45	2·73	5·41	2·56	7·99
8 ,, ...	23°	97·40	132·11	135·92	109·37	2·70	5·35	2·54	7·91
9 ,, ...	23°	97·39	132·07	135·90	109·31	2·69	5·31	2·52	7·85
17 ,, ...	24°	97·36	131·95	135·85	109·10	2·66	5·19	2·47	7·64
24 ,, ...	23°	97·36	131·92	135·835	109·03	2·66	5·16	2·455	7·57
30 ,, ...	23°	97·38	131·92	135·83	108·99	2·68	5·16	2·45	7·53
7 Dec. ...	21°	97·39	131·90	135·81	108·95	2·69	5·14	2·43	7·49
14 ,, ...	25°	97·40	131·92	135·815	108·95	2·70	5·16	2·435	7·49
21 ,, ...	24°	97·40	131·93	135·815	108·94	2·70	5·17	2·435	7·48
28 ,, ...	22°	97·41	131·933	135·818	108·93	2·71	5·173	2·438	7·47
1903 18 Jan. ...	23°	97·42	131·96	135·83	108·93	2·72	5·20	2·45	7·47
14 Feb. ...	22°	97·42	132·00	135·845	108·95	2·72	5·24	2·465	7·49
12 April ...	23°	97·43	132·02	135·85	108·96	2·73	5·26	2·47	7·50
2 June ...	23°	97·44	132·05	135·87	109·01	2·74	5·29	2·49	7·55
11 Oct. ...	25°	97·46	132·07	135·875	109·02	2·76	5·31	2·495	7·56
31 Dec. ...	22°	97·47	132·07	135·878	109·035	2·77	5·31	2·498	7·575
1904 23 May ...	22°	97·49	132·105	135·89	109·08	2·79	5·345	2·51	7·62

of Four Varnishes.

LOSS.							
By Evaporation.				Per cent. on Original Weight.			
No. 1.	No. 2.	No. 3.	No. 4.	No. 1.	No. 2.	No. 3.	No. 4.
...	...	...	...	...	...	...	...
...	...	...	...	...	...	...	...
1·20	·96	·60	1·23	29·27	14·29	18·07	12·60
·10	·19	·10	·30	2·44	2·83	3·01	3·07,
·04	·095	·03	·14	·98	1·41	·90	1·43
·03	·065	·03	·11	·73	·97	·90	1·12
·03	·06	·02	·08	·73	·89	·60	·82
·01	·04	·02	·06	·24	·59	·60	·61
·03	·12	·05	·21	·73	1·79	1·51	2·15
...	·03	·015	·07	...	·44	·45	·72
...	·00	·005	·04	...	·00	·15	·41
...	·02	·02	·04	..	·30	·60	·41
...	...ı	...	·00	...	...	...	·00
...	...	...	·01	...	...	...	·10
...	...	...	·01	...	...	...	·10
1·44	1·58	·89	2·30	35·12	23·51	26·79	23·54
TOTAL LOSS.				TOTAL LOSS.			
GAIN on minimum.				GAIN per cent. on minimum weight.			
·13	·205	·08	·15	4·89	3·97	3·30	2·01

a little too low.   This consideration introduces complication into
the problem, but cannot materially influence the main conclusions
to be drawn from the facts.

      *   *   *   *   *   *

In the production of oil-varnish, whether the resin ingredient be
natural or artificial, some interesting problems introduce themselves.
These soon attracted my attention, and during the preparation of such
varnishes I was constantly on the alert for any clue that might lead
to their solution.   Close observation added very little to the known
facts, however; but a little enlightenment on some of the factors
involved now enables probable explanations to be suggested.

The direct heat to which copal is subjected to promote its
solubility leads to very uncertain results; the evident object of
the operator is to fuse the fossil resin without allowing much time
for dehydration.   Fusion alone is not what happens to the resin;
it splits into a volatile hydrocarbon and a colophone; the solubility
and brown colour of this latter substance depend upon the unknown
extent of its dehydration.

The case with the artificial resins is very much the same when
a sand-bath or other direct-heating method is employed—brown
colour results from decomposition and the extent of dehydration
is an unknown quantity; but temperatures not exceeding 100° C.
appear to have no effect except to cause dehydration, while the
extent of this may be approximately estimated from the degree
of oxidation and the duration of a fairly constant temperature.

Experience leads me to suppose that persistent degradation
(substitution of one atom of oxygen for two of hydrogen) of a
terpene hydrocarbon is attended by constantly decreasing solubility
in oil of turpentine and linseed-oil; by increasing solubility in
aqueous alcohol, as well as affinity for oxygen.

Oxy-terpenes, which have lost little hydrogen, are readily
soluble in both oil of turpentine and linseed-oil; consequently the
proportions of the varnish are determined by considerations quite
apart from solution; but with loss of hydrogen they become less
and less soluble in these menstrua as they become more viscous

(an indication of degradation); a point is soon reached when solution in oil of turpentine alone becomes impracticable.

At this stage, the practical mode of proceeding is to dissolve the fused resin in hot linseed-oil, afterwards to cautiously dilute this solution (whose temperature is maintained) with oil of turpentine. As the resin becomes more viscous (by degradation) precautions in diluting need to be increased; at first cold oil of turpentine may be gradually introduced, later on it must be warmed, finally it must be raised to nearly the same temperature as the varnish.

It will soon be observed that if the diluent is added a little too quickly precipitation of resin will ensue (this is a hint that dilution must be restricted); at the commencement of the diluting process, this precipitate may be again dissolved by constant mixing and the maintenance of temperature—no permanent harm will be done; but such want of care must not occur towards the completion of dilution or the precipitation will be permanent—the varnish will be spoilt; the whole of the operations must be repeated with new materials.

If the making of the varnish has been successfully completed, it must be mixed together as it cools. The resulting cold varnish should be clear as crystal. Once completed and cooled, its viscosity can neither be increased nor diminished by evaporation or dilution. A few drops of cold turpentine added to it will immediate cause precipitation. Raised most cautiously to the temperature at which it was diluted, a little oil of turpentine of equal temperature is added; while hot the operation appears to be successful, but as the varnish cools it becomes turbid and breaks up (" le vernis louche ").

The perplexing point is that as the solution of resin in oil becomes more viscous, appearing to require more oil of turpentine to bring it to a convenient consistency, the constitution of the varnish demands a diminution of the diluent instead of an increase; supposing always that the proportion of oil remains constant.

Experts judge of the sufficiency of oil in a copal varnish by testing a drop of the oil solution cooled on a plate of cold glass; this is an attempt to produce constancy of viscosity at this stage. The old violin-makers appear to have maintained the proportion of oil nearly constant, preferring to attempt to manipulate a thick varnish rather than diminish its effect and brilliancy.

The explanation suggested to account for these complex phenomena is that, in accordance with the usual laws, the solubility of the solid in the liquids increases with rise of temperature; it decreases as the resemblance of its chemical composition to that of the solvents becomes less. As dehydration of the resin increases (of which viscosity and deepening colour are the signs), a point is soon reached when its solubility in oil of turpentine becomes very small; linseed-oil then is the efficient solvent, oil of turpentine its diluent, both menstrua being miscible. When the quantity of solvent employed is greater than that required to produce a saturated solution, its dilution will be practicable to an extent dependent upon the margin of superfluity; it will follow that, if with a given resin convenient proportions of oil and essence are known, an increase of its dehydration, which reduces its solubility, will demand either an increase of oil or a decrease of essence: if the solvent remains a constant, the dilution must decrease; if the quantity of diluent is constant, the solvent must increase.

The complexity of the problem is aided by the fact that the small amount of solvent action of the oil of turpentine still further decreases as well as that of the more efficient solvent—linseed-oil.

Since solution takes place at a comparatively high temperature, about 100° C. and upwards, it may be supposed that, in many cases, oil-varnishes may be, when cool, supersaturated solutions; it is known that they generally require mixing during the cooling process.

This explanation must be admitted to be plausible even if its absolute correctness may be questioned; in any case it cannot account for the fact that, after a varnish is successfully completed and cooled, its viscosity cannot be modified either by evaporation (if too thin) or by further dilution (if too thick); this critical condition must be quite apart from the question of saturation. If a varnish is too thick this defect may be remedied by making another varnish, under identical conditions, but with an increase of diluent (a demonstration that in that particular case the point of saturation was not reached); when cool, the two varnishes may be mixed together. But if an attempt be made to add a little cold oil of turpentine to the varnish, precipitation ensues, or if it is most carefully raised to a proper temperature for dilution, and the wanting increment of diluent be most cautiously added, when the varnish cools it breaks up ("le vernis louche"). This is a mystery as to which experts offer no enlightenment.

The observed phenomena make it quite clear that this critical condition of a varnish after completion cannot be dependent on solution; it must result from some change in one or more of its constituents consequent on re-heating, or which has already taken place, and becomes apparent when this is attempted. The influence of moderate heat on the resin has already, it is hoped, been made sufficiently plain; in many cases the solution of resin in oil has, previous to dilution, been heated for many hours at 100° C. without affecting its constitution; it is therefore most improbable that it should be materially affected by sufficient re-heating (over a water-bath) to bring it again to about the same temperature. The part of the varnish which undergoes change or exhibits its effects on re-heating is manifestly the oil of turpentine used for dilution. It has already been demonstrated that a part only of this oil of turpentine is eventually spontaneously evaporated from a pellicle of varnish; it has been constantly observed that when oil of turpentine is mixed with a varnish at 100° its characteristic odour soon disappears. The only reasonable inference which it appears possible to draw from all these facts is that, when the pinene is brought into intimate contact with the other ingredients of the varnish at 100°, it undergoes some change in structure; when re-heated it splits; as it does when it is oxidized, to a very moderate degree, with nitric acid, and (after the completion of the oxidation reaction) is subjected to a temperature of 100° or upwards, the distillate being a hydrocarbon which differs from the original dextro-pinene in being either lævo-rotatory or optically inactive, while the residue is no longer volatile.

*   *   *   *   *   *

As to the question of the old varnishes, I have been forced to abandon the old dogma in favour of a new one, which rests upon

v.   6

evidence so satisfactory in every direction that I adopt it without hesitation; but as to the chemistry of the terpenes, while many of the doctrines taught by much esteemed teachers are now apparently untenable, no new faith supported by sufficient evidence has been formulated.

M. Berthelot obtained derivatives from oil of turpentine which were often of two kinds: *e.g.*, artificial camphor, solid and fluid. He observed dichröism in some of his products, but offered no explanation. He derived lævo- from dextro-oil of turpentine by subjecting it to temperatures above 250° C. from 2 to 60 hours (39, 10 and 11). He attributed these phenomena to isomerism.

While isomerism is readily admitted, it seems insufficient to account for all the observed facts; my poor efforts to ascertain the presence of isomerides in dextro-pinene have been unavailing; it appears to be perfectly homogeneous when well and carefully rectified.

The facts which have come under my notice point rather to asymmetry in the terpenes or to phenomena which resemble those attending the inversion of sugar.

A few of the points which appear to be significant are here briefly stated:—

When oil of turpentine (dextro-pinene is always to be understood) is oxygenated it is invariably found to contain ozone.

Oil of turpentine readily forms hydrates, but the derived hydrocarbon (terebene), whether lævo or inactive, does not form them (experiments which I have made on this point simply confirm those of more competent observers).

When oil of turpentine is oxidized, even by the most gentle means, it is evident that (at least) two products are formed, the one resinous, the other fluid and volatile; the lævo-rotation of the latter approximates very closely to one-half of the dextro-rotation of the original pinene; its affinity for oxygen is quite different from that of the original fluid, as may be easily observed by the behaviour of the two substances with nitric acid. The appearance of dichröism at the moment of separation of the component parts of the pinene seems peculiarly significant.

In no case has it been found possible to transform the whole of the oil of turpentine either into resin or into an isomeric volatile oil: it always yields both solid and volatile products.

The optical changes which may be observed in the terpenes are not more remarkable than those which affect the olfactory nerves. The odour of oil of turpentine is too characteristic to be mistaken; when pinene is transformed into nitro-pinene this odour disappears and is replaced by another which is characteristic of pine- or fir-wood (here is a fact of singular significance); when the nitro-pinene is decomposed, the oxy-pinene has a pleasant aromatic scent; on distillation, a fluid of an agreeable ethereal odour is obtained, the residue is aromatic.

The mere mixing of oil of turpentine with a solution of oxy-terpene in linseed-oil, at 100°, appears to determine a change in its constitution; its characteristic odour is changed, a part of it evaporates spontaneously, the residue persists in the pellicle and apparently becomes slowly oxidized.

The changes in solubility, which have been described as occurring when oil of turpentine is oxidized by natural means (Mailand), when it is oxidized by nitric alcohol or by nitric acid, when the resulting oxide splits, when copal splits under the influence of heat, when colophony splits or is divided into two parts, &c., are not without interest.

All these observed transformations point to change of molecular construction, the determination of which is beyond the scope of the present research and of its author. It is to be hoped that experienced scientific chemists, having sufficient time at their disposal, will take up the study of the terpenes and enlighten the scientific world on their constitutions and their mysterious modifications, natural and artificial.

CHAPTER 7

CONCLUSION

In order to form some definite conception of the general characteristics of the varnishes of the old violin-makers, the only practicable method (for persons who have not unlimited time at their disposal) is to study the descriptions given by experts, whose vocation has given them opportunities for examining many examples of the work of the different masters, or by musicians (professional or amateur) whose enthusiasm has led them to take an intelligent interest in the instruments on which they have played or which have come under their notice.

Some quotations have already been given from acknowledged authorities; if these are read, with or without reference to the voluminous and discursive literature on the subject, one idea will be found to be generally prevalent—viz., that the old Italian varnishes, covering musical instruments, were something special, different from those which are found in the world on other articles; that they had a common basis peculiar to themselves. Mr. Hart writes:—" Every instrument belonging to the school of Cremona " has it, more or less, in all its marvellous beauty " (35). . . . " These varnishes " (Brescian, Cremonese, Neapolitan and Venetian) " are quite separable in one particular, which is the depth of their " colouring; and yet three of them, the Brescian, Cremonese, and " Venetian, have to all appearance a common basis." . . . " If we " examine the Brescian varnish, we find an almost complete " resemblance between the material of Gaspard di Salo and that " of his coadjutors, the colouring only being different. Upon " turning to the Cremonese, we find that Joseph Guarnerius, " Stradiuarius, Carlo Bergonzi and a few others used varnish " having the same characteristics, but again different in shade; " possibly the method of laying it upon the instrument was peculiar " to each maker. Similar facts are observable in the Venetian " specimens. The varnish of Naples, again, is of a totally different

" composition, and as it was chiefly in vogue after the Cremonese
" was lost, we may conclude that it was probably produced by the
" Neapolitan makers for their own need." (36.)

There seems therefore to have been a continuity in the basis of
the varnish from the time of Gasparo da Salo, in the early part of
the sixteenth century, down to that of Stradivari and his pupils,
in the middle of the eighteenth—roughly, for about two centuries.
The Neapolitan was a later product; it is not quite clear whether
it is recognized as a relation of the family or not.

If, as Mr. Hart supposes, this basis was a gum, common at the
time, used for other purposes besides that of covering musical
instruments, it is not a little remarkable that it should have been
found in localities so far apart, politically and geographically, as
Brescia and Cremona were from Venice (communications were
neither easy nor rapid in those days), and yet should not be
mentioned by one of the authors quoted by M. Mailand in his
research.

Then Mr. Hart gives in a few words a description of the
characteristic colours:—" The Brescian is mostly of a rich brown
" colour and soft texture, but not so clear as the Cremonese. The
" Cremonese is of various shades, the early instruments of the
" school being chiefly amber-coloured, afterwards deepening into
" a light red of charming appearance; later still into a rich brown
" of the Brescian type, though more transparent, and frequently
" broken up, while the earlier kinds are velvet-like. The Venetian
" is also of various shades, chiefly light red, and exceedingly
" transparent. The Neapolitan varnish (a generic term including
" that of Milan and a few other places) is very clear, and chiefly
" yellow in colour, but wanting the dainty softness of the
" Cremonese." (38.)

Reference to the writings of other authorities enables some
of the details of this sketch to be filled in. The Messrs. Hill
write:—" We may thus fairly assume that Stradivari was at an
" early stage of his career initiated into the traditions and methods
" practised by his master and predecessors. Once freed from his
" connection with Amati, we see him seeking, by changes effected
" in the colours of his varnish, to give a different appearance to

" his instruments, as is evidenced by his departure from the hitherto
" conventional Amati yellow. We say ' conventional,' because,
" throughout the four generations of that remarkable family,
" every member of it kept, with rare exceptions, to the same tint
" of colour." (Stradivari. 174.) We learn from this that the
Amati used varnish of a yellow colour for four generations; that
Stradivari did not depart from the old traditions, as to varnish,
until his connection with Nicolo Amati was broken by his death
in 1684. Stradivari designed the " Long Strad " in 1690; he
returned to Amati traditions, as to form, in 1698. It is as rational
to assume that Stradivari changed his varnish for the sake of the
appearance of his instruments as it would be to assume that he
changed their form for the same reason; a motive must be sought
which is more consistent with the character of this eminent man
and with the steady purpose of his life and work.

M. Fétis fixes for us the epoch of change, and also expresses
in felicitous terms his view of the aim of his long life. He writes
(the translation is mine):—" In 1700, the artist has reached his
" fifty-sixth year. His talent is then in its full strength; the
" instruments which leave his hands, from this time up to 1725,
" are so many perfect works. He no longer feels his way. Certain
" of what he does, he carries into the smallest details the most
" beautiful finish. His model has all desirable amplitude; he
" draws the contours of it with a taste, a purity, which for a century
" and a half have excited the admiration of connoisseurs." . . .
" The beautiful warm tones of the varnish of Stradivari date from
" this epoch. Its body is fine and of great elasticity." (Vol. VIII.,
152.) . . .

" Stradivari belonged to that small number of those eminent
" men (hommes d'élite) who, setting up for themselves as their
" end and aim, perfection (so far as is given to humanity to attain
" it), do not allow themselves to stray from the path which may
" lead them to it; whom nothing distracts, nothing deflects from
" their object; whom deceptions do not discourage, and who,
" full of faith in the value of their object as in their abilities to
" realize it, incessantly recommence whatever they have done well,
" in order to arrive at the best possible. For Stradivari, violin-

" making was the whole world; he concentrated in it the whole of
" his personality. This is the way to rise to eminence, when
" aptitude answers to will." (153.)

The distinguishing attribute of Stradivari, after he had passed
his youth and had reached the prime of his mental capacity, is his
thoughtfulness: no detail of form or of construction escaped the
most minute consideration. To suppose that he overlooked the
influence of varnish on the tone of his instruments, as well as on
their appearance, can only arise from ignorance of the chemical
and physical problems involved; it may be taken as certain that
he devoted time and thought to the study of this question as well
as of all others that were factors affecting the attainment of his
ideal perfection.

After 1725 the varnish of Stradivari tended more towards shades
of brown (this change could not have been without reason); this
tendency is observable not only in his instruments, but also in
those of other makers living at that time, some of whom were his
pupils and other most probably cognisant of his opinions. A
quotation has already been given from M. Vidal in which he describes
the varnishes of the pupils of Stradivari as more heavy, thick, and
red-brown. In his opinion, this is an indication of the commencement of decline.

It will now not be difficult, from the descriptions and opinions
of the various experts, to construct the probable course of evolution
of the Brescian-Cremonese varnish; the makers of these two towns
(not far distant from each other) appear to have had much mutual
influence. The earliest examples of Brescia were brown, a little
wanting in transparency; the earliest Cremonese were mostly yellow
or amber-coloured, more transparent than those of Brescia. Deeper
colours began to appear some time after 1684; the warm tones of
Stradivari about 1700; after 1725 brown shades (which do not seem
at any period to have been entirely absent) were again introduced;
the varnish finally disappeared about 1750. The Brescian varnishes
were very soft; those of Cremona had a " dainty softness "; some
of the varnishes of Stradivari appear to have had a tendency towards
hardness—were a little " chippy."

The Venetian varnishes were of various tints, resembling those of Cremona—often light red. No facts as to their evolution are available; but, apparently, they excelled all others in transparency. Mr. Hart's expression is "exceedingly transparent."

The Neapolitan varnishes were mostly yellow, but (as I know from my own experience) they were sometimes of a red-brown colour, which is more garish than the warm tints of the Cremonese and Venetian types. The yellow varnishes were "very clear," but the red ones were wanting in perfect transparency. In general they were harder than the Cremonese and Venetian.

The assumption that the common basis of all the varnishes was a gum is rejected; it is assumed that the old violin-makers used as the resinous ingredients of their varnishes the products of the coniferous trees which grew in their vicinity.

A simple and almost obvious explanation is suggested for the slight difference between the Brescian-Cremonese and the Venetian varnishes:—It is well known that turpentine derived from larch (Larix Europæa) has for centuries been an article of commerce from Venice; large products are therefore allotted to Venice, and those of the pines and firs (Pinus, Abies, and Picea) to Brescia and Cremona. We adopt the purely arbitrary distinction of calling varnishes derived from fir- or pine-turpentine, galipot, rosin or colophony—Cremonese; those derived from Venice turpentine— Venetian. We soon find, by experiment, that the characteristics of these two kinds of varnish correspond closely with those ascribed to the two districts. Both yield similar varieties of colour, but there is a small difference in shade—the Venetian is slightly more trans- parent, and is a little harder when perfectly dry.

M. Mailand cites only two authors who wrote in the sixteenth century, Alexis the Piedmontese (1550) and Fioravanti (Bologna, 1564). Piedmont is a little remote from our scene; Bologna is nearer. Alexis prescribes "turpentine of Venice"; also "pine "resin, fat and white" (galipot). Fioravanti prescribes pine oil (perhaps crude turpentine, not of oil of turpentine as M. Mailand suggests); Greek pitch (resin from the pine trees of Calabria); pine resin. At the present time there is no difficulty in obtaining turpentine of Venice, which is still in commerce; instead of the various pine products of Italy, it is now more convenient to use those in commerce which come from ports in or near the Gulf of Mexico (from regions where the climate much resembles that of Italy)—viz., colophony and oil of turpentine.

In order to obtain resins suitable for the production of fine varnish, these various substances require oxidation. It requires no advanced student of chemistry to discern that the varnishes on the old instruments are products of oxidation; thus much I had settled in my mind many years before this research was contemplated. What oxidant was employed in the old days there is no means of knowing. That which has been found to be eminently suited to the purpose is nitric acid, which has the inestimable advantage of leaving nothing behind it—it parts with a portion or the whole of its oxygen to the turpentine or colophony; the residuary nitrogen, or its lower oxides, and water are easily perfectly eliminated by heat.

Nitric acid, as the oxidant, affords a simple and complete explanation for the evolution of all the different types of varnish. Some other oxidant may enable an equally plausible explanation to be given, but I must confess that I am not able to suggest what it could be.

There can be no possible doubt that nitric acid (called then spirit of nitre) was easily obtainable in the sixteenth century; it had been known since the eighth. It was in those days derived from nitre (potassic nitrate), nitrate of soda being not then abundantly available as it is to-day.

The oxidation of the turpentines is indispensable; the source of the oxygen is in no way material. Turpentine may have been found in Italy sufficiently oxidized by natural processes; the Greek pitch from the conifers of Calabria, mentioned by Fioravanti and Bonanni, is possibly a product of this kind. The oxygenating powers of oil of turpentine may have been utilized; if so, it must have been a slow process indeed. Finally, nitric acid or some other artificial oxidant may have been employed. The discovery of the oxidant actually used would be most interesting; in the meantime, nitric acid is so satisfactory in every respect that it cannot easily be excelled.

When Gasparo came from Salo to Brescia he must have known

resin or colophony, for it is essential to the friction of the hair
of a bow on a string. Very probably this substance was the first
used for a varnish also.

If a good sample of colophony be oxidized to a moderate extent,
a brilliant resin of an intense yellow colour, very much resembling
gamboge, will be obtained. This resin is completely soluble in
oil of turpentine; consequently a varnish may be produced from
it without any admixture of linseed-oil. When an instrument
has been covered with this varnish, its appearance will be satisfactory
in every respect: the ground tone will be amber-yellow, the refractions
caused by the grain of the wood will be of a red colour; but
when this varnish dries (in a month or six weeks), it will be found
to be wanting in sufficient cohesion to bear wear or polishing.

There are two obvious remedies for this defect: the first is to
introduce into the varnish a proportion of thick raw turpentine;
the second, a similar introduction of boiled linseed-oil. With the
experience of the varnish-makers of a century at my disposal, I
did not hesitate to adopt the second expedient as the best; but
it by no means follows that, had I lived in the sixteenth century,
I should have taken the same course; from the facts at our disposal,
it would appear that the early makers of Brescia adopted the
first expedient.

The most obvious means, then, for forming a varnish from the
yellow resin would be to dissolve it in crude turpentine by the
aid of a charcoal brazier or a similar direct-heating appliance,
keeping the ingredients well stirred with a wooden spatula or rod.
The effect of this operation would be to cause dehydration, as
well as a little decomposition, of the yellow resin; the resulting
varnish would be of a brown colour—pale, if the heating had been
moderate; of a deeper shade if the heating had been extended in
duration or in degree. If the varnish were made cold, which
would require some time, the colour would be yellow.

When an instrument had been covered with this transparent
yellow or brown varnish, and after the volatile part of the turpentine
had slowly and spontaneously evaporated, the remaining pellicle
would be a pure resin, modified by oxide of turpentine; such a
varnish would exactly answer the description given by M. Fétis

of the varnish of G. P. Maggini—" a pale brown spirit varnish ":
for it would be completely soluble in alcohol.

It will be easily understood, from what has been already stated,
that such a turpentine varnish would be more transparent if pale.

These turpentine varnishes represent the early varnishes of
Brescia (perhaps of Cremona).

It is conceivable that in the hands of men of the high intelligence
of the old Brescian and Cremonese masters, whose powers of
observation had been cultivated and increased by long study of
technical (not to say scientific) problems, the defects of the method
of production and of the finished varnish would soon become
apparent. The introduction of linseed-oil would be the first obvious
improvement in the durability and cohesion of the pellicle. It
has already been demonstrated by M. Mailand that methods for
the necessary transformation of raw into boiled oil were known
in the time of Maggini.

This improvement, still accompanied by the application of
direct heat, would explain the manufacture of oil-varnish such
as that used on the later instruments of Maggini; on those of the
earlier makers of Cremona; and, up to a much later date, on those
of Italian makers, who were not very particular about the colour
and quality of their varnish. The tints would be varying shades
of golden brown with red and red-brown refractions.

The uncertainty of result caused by difficulty in controlling the
direct mode of heating must soon have led to the use of the water-
bath (the " balneum mariæ " of the old chemists). It is impossible
to say how early this simple device was known; Alexis prescribes
its use in 1550; Zahn in 1685. The introduction of this improvement
would lead at once to greater certainty in the manufacture: degree
of temperature (100°) would now be a constant, the factor movable
at will, duration. Not only this, the brown colour, due to the action
on the varnish of the over-heated surface of the containing vessel,
would disappear; instead of the brown tones of the early period,
the yellow and orange colours, with red refractions, of the Amati,
would now appear; the ultimate production of the warm tones of
Stradivari's great epoch would be a question of evolution. From
the examination of about a dozen instruments of Stradivari and

from the representations of a few others, I conclude that this painstaking workman invariably used the water-bath in preparing his varnish.

The influence of the colour and character of the wood on the apparent colour of the varnish is greater than one could conceive possible. It is intelligible when the effect of complicated reflection, from varying planes, is well understood; but even then the practical results are often surprising.

The effect of these varnishes on the wood of the belly or table is eminently characteristic. In forming the moulding of this important part of the instrument (especially of the smaller ones), the angle of section of the grain is constantly changing, thus bringing into view, more or less, the medullary rays. Moreover, the absorption of varnish is greater where the tiny cylindrical fibres have been cut across. This variation of section, under the refracting varnish, produces the mottled appearance which Mr. Hart so truthfully describes. The beautiful satin-like appearance of some of the tables is remarkable, considering that they are made of wood so apparently devoid of character as that of Abies or Picea.

From what has been said, it will be understood how it happens that, among the works of the old masters, no two instruments are alike. The variations in the varnish itself are infinite (it seems unlikely that they prepared any considerable quantity at one time); difference in the proportion of nitric acid, in the duration of nitrification, in the duration and method of heating, must have produced unlimited variety. The effect was further greatly modified by the quality and character of the wood.

No doubt age has, to a small extent, changed the colour of the old instruments; but this change, which is not material, is not to be attributed to modification of the varnish, but to the wood. All woody tissue has a tendency to become brown with age—even the practically pure cellulose of paper has a decided tendency in this direction. The apparent colour of the old instruments is therefore to-day somewhat deeper than when they left the hands of their makers; always supposing that the thickness of the pellicle has remained practically constant, and that it has not been unduly exposed to direct sunlight.

If this hypothetical and manifestly imperfect sketch (for how little reliable material is to be found when it is tested !) of the old varnishes (from their origin until Stradivari had reached his prime) has any solid foundation, it may be supposed that when once in the course of this research the true starting-point had been reached, the evolution of the varnishes, in my hands, would follow the same course as in the old days. The Italians were working in the dark—they could not have known the significance of their simple operations; while I had some knowledge of modern chemical laws and theory to enlighten my task. For this reason—not from any inferior natural acumen—the slow evolution in their hands extended over two centuries, while in mine it occupied only as many years. As I proceeded, every varnish which indicated a new phase of evolution was laid on an instrument, to enable progress to be clearly appreciated. The modern evolution is thus illustrated by a collection of little more than a score of instruments; the ancient one was spread over many thousands.

In order that my readers may be able to follow the gradual evolution and appreciate its significance, from the earliest Brescian varnishes down to the masterpieces of Stradivari, I will give, as concisely as possible, the exact dates on which the different varnishes were prepared. The different processes have already been sufficiently described in detail.

The Neapolitan varnishes will be intentionally omitted, because their mode of production became prematurely known to me from circumstances which have already been fully explained.

Although dichröism had been observed in May, and the identity of the colours of oxidized pitch-pine with those of the old varnishes had been discerned in June, it was not until the end of November, 1900, that experiment and investigation enabled me to conclude with certainty that these phenomena were due to the presence of oxides of turpentine and their derivatives. This preliminary investigation was not without interest, but the facts brought to light are scarcely relevant to the present question.

The preparation of turpentine varnishes (without linseed-oil) extended from the 30th December, 1900, to the 19th January, 1901. The earliest of these varnishes were yellow; the later .

yellow-brown. These represent the earlier varnishes of Brescia, which M. Fétis supposed to be spirit varnishes; the pellicles were perfectly soluble in aqueous alcohol (about 90 per cent.).

After testing the last of these varnishes, I concluded that they were wanting in cohesion; I therefore determined on the admixture of siccative linseed-oil. It is now a matter of great regret to me that I removed these pure turpentine varnishes from the violins which I covered with them; slips of wood varnished with them, at the same time, show that the varnish has gradually solidified.

The first oil-varnish was made from colophony (in the dry way), over a sand-bath, on the 31st January, 1901; a perfectly successful oil-varnish made in this way was prepared on the 13th February, 1901. A violin was coated with this varnish; the colour is a peculiar golden yellow-brown, with brown shadows and red-brown refractions; it very much resembles that of the " Dumas " violin made by G. P. Maggini, the back of which is represented in colours in the book of Messrs. Hill (Maggini 61), but it does not exactly correspond with the tints of the drawing.

Several other varnishes were made in the same way with the sand-bath; but I soon realized that this mode of heating was too uncertain. Some fine varnishes were made, others were spoilt by too high a temperature; in all cases they were of a brown tone. Deep-brown varnish made with the sand-bath requires too much oil for solution to suit my ideal. This mode of heating was abandoned; henceforth the water-bath and water-oven were used instead.

The first oil-varnish (made in the wet way), from colophony dissolved in oil of turpentine, with the water-bath, was prepared on the 19th February, 1901. A violin was coated with this; it is pale yellow with light red refractions. The quality leaves nothing to be desired, but it is rather too pale to be effective.

On the 21st February, 1901, a similar varnish was made from turpentine of Venice; a violin was covered with it. A varnish of the finest quality—golden yellow, with red-brown refractions. This Venetian varnish is much more effective than the corresponding Cremonese; as a pale varnish, it leaves absolutely nothing to be desired.

On the 17th March, 1901, a varnish was made from colophony dissolved in oil of turpentine, similar to the last Cremonese varnish; it was heated over a water-bath for five hours. The increased depth of colour and viscosity were observed; it was conjectured that the changes caused by this heating signified " dehydration." This varnish was used for a violin and a viola; it is a good varnish of the Amati type—perfectly transparent, brilliant, golden yellow with red-brown refractions; agreeing exactly with the description which Cartier gave of that on the violins made by Andrea Amati for the King of France, which has already been quoted; its tint exactly matches that of early varnishes of Stradivari.

Considerable time was now spent on endeavouring to determine interesting theoretical questions.

On the 27th April, 1901, a Cremonese varnish was made similar to the last, but of a deeper colour (oxidation and dehydration both increased). A violin and violoncello were covered with it; colour, orange with red-brown refractions.

On the 24th May, 1901, a Venetian varnish was prepared, which was used for two violins, the one of which exhibited a fine orange-red colour, the other inclining more to orange-brown shades. The reason for this difference was that the first violin had been previously covered with a Cremonese varnish, which had been removed by alcohol; the second was a virgin violin. A very transparent varnish of perfect quality, it solidifies to a slightly harder pellicle than a corresponding Cremonese varnish.

On the 4th September, 1901, a Cremonese varnish (C), a Venetian varnish (V), were made on precisely similar lines; they were both used for violins, both exhibiting the orange-red tones of Stradivari. Both varnishes were of excellent quality, but the Venetian was judged to be slightly superior in colour, transparency, and brilliancy. The Venetian pellicle was decidedly harder than the other.

On the 29th November, 1901, a Venetian varnish was made, and a violoncello was covered with it. This varnish answers the description given by M. de Try of that on the Stradivari violoncello of 1725, on which he had played in Madrid; it is a very transparent varnish, of an amber-yellow colour with bright red refractions.

At this stage I observed the effect caused by prolonged nitrification on oxidation.

On the 9th December, 1901, two Cremonese varnishes were made precisely alike up to the oxidation stage (nitrification extended over four days); the one was subsequently heated for a short time only in the water-oven, the other for six hours; the one was not perceptibly, the other was considerably, dehydrated. One was used for a violin, the other for a viola. That on the violin is of a bright yellow colour with copper-coloured refractions; the dehydrated one on the viola is deep orange with red-brown refractions. Both are very good, but perhaps not quite so effective as Venetian varnishes.

Finally, on the 25th April, 1902, a varnish was made from equal parts of Venice turpentine and oil of turpentine. Nitrification was extended over three weeks; consequently oxidation was probably the maximum possible at one operation. A violin was covered with this varnish: a transparent, brilliant varnish of a deep orange-red, the most coloured Venetian varnish in my collection (it was, of course, hybrid, for a considerable part of the oil of turpentine was oxidized).

As far as I am aware, this last varnish exhausted my powers of evolution (not of variety) of Cremonese and Venetian varnishes, consistent with the maintenance of my ideal of quality; of varnishes of declining quality I shall write later.

In the month of August, 1902, the Messrs. Hill published their book on Stradivari; my copy reached me about the twenty-fifth day of that month. This book contains excellent representations of some of the finest instruments of Stradivari in existence. After examining these coloured drawings (since I have practised water-colour drawing for nearly half a century, my eye—whatever natural defect it may have—cannot be considered untrained), I sought in my collection of instruments for examples which might possibly match them. Somewhat to my surprise, I found that, in almost every case, I possessed instruments which corresponded exactly, or very closely indeed, with the tints of the drawings. It is necessary that I should express myself clearly on this point: what I mean to assert is that, if I gave a commission to a water-colour artist to depict my instruments, I should consider that he acquitted himself very well indeed if he came as near as the tints in the book. The backs only of the instruments were taken as a guide; the tables are always more or less modified by resin, &c.

Here are the instruments of Stradivari and the dates they bear, with the corresponding dates on which I made the varnishes, the tints of which match the plates:—

Long Pattern Strad. Violin	...	1693	Page 48		17 March, 1901.
Inlaid Viola	...	1696	,, 108		17 March, 1901.
Tuscan Strad. Violin	...	1690	,, 164	(C)	4 Sept., 1901.
Duport Strad. Violoncello	...	1711	,, 144		24 May, 1901.
Rode Strad. Violin ...	...	1722	,, 238	(V)	4 Sept., 1901.
Alard Strad. Violin ...	...	1715	,, 90		25 April, 1902.

It will be also remembered that M. de Try described a varnish on a Strad. violoncello of 1725, the similar varnish to which I made on the 29th November, 1901.

Soon after, I acquired a copy of Mr. A. J. Hipkins' book, and on applying the same test to the drawings therein I found an exact match for the

Hellier Strad. Violin ... 1679 Plate XXV. 27 April, 1901.

The Alard Strad. violin and the King Joseph Guarnerius del Gesu violin, on Plate XXVI., I am unable to match; although, curiously enough, I can match the Alard Strad. violin as depicted by the Messrs. Hill.

Of the instruments pictured by the Messrs Hill, I had seen one, the " Tuscan Strad." violin, about fifteen years before, I possessed their coloured illustration (dated 1889) of this instrument; the others I had never seen, neither was I aware of their existence.

It has already been distinctly stated that it is impossible for anyone to know beforehand the exact colour which an instrument will exhibit when coated with a varnish (such as those whose method of production I have described); consequently, there can be no question here of copying what I had never seen; the matching of the tints is a pure coincidence. In the case of my Venetian varnish of the 24th May, 1901, as I have related, two violins were covered with this varnish, one of which matched the colour of the Duport violoncello, the other not resembling it. The reason for the great difference in colour between these two violins, covered with the same varnish, did not for some time occur to me. I attributed it at first to the different character of the wood; afterwards I remembered that one of these violins had been coated with a Cremonese varnish, which, not being entirely satisfactory, was removed by the aid of methylated alcohol. This was the violin which, when afterwards covered with the Venetian varnish, matched the colour of the Duport violoncello. Now, although it is not very difficult to remove a varnish from the surface of an instrument, that with which the wood is saturated cannot be removed; consequently, when this wood was subsequently coated with another varnish, the result may be said to constitute a kind of hybrid between the Cremonese and Venetian varieties, the latter largely preponderating. The soundness of this hypothesis was demonstrated, in March, 1903, when I prepared a varnish whose turpentine constituents were 100 parts turpentine of Venice, 17 parts of oil of turpentine, 5 parts of colophony; with this hybrid varnish I coated a violoncello whose wood resembled that of the Duport Strad., and, as I expected, I obtained an almost exact replica of this instrument.

My varnish of the 25th April, 1902, was made from equal parts of turpentine of Venice and of oil of turpentine (a sample of a yellow tinge that would be sure to yield a considerable proportion of resin by oxidation); this was therefore again a hybrid varnish, which matched the colour of the Alard Strad. violin of 1715 (Hill).

Attention is not called to these facts from a desire to prejudge the question of the identity of the modern with the ancient varnish, but because the different tints revealed interesting deductions which were totally unexpected, which will now be explained.

If it be assumed, for the present purpose, that Stradivari was experimenting with varnishes identical with the modern ones, it is not at all difficult to classify the varnishes on the various instruments (judging only by the tints):—

The Long Pattern Violin (1693)	
The Inlaid Viola (1696)	Cremonese varnish.
The Tuscan Violin (1690)	
The Hillier Violin (1679)	

The Rode Violin (1722)	
The Madrid Violoncello (1725)	Venetian varnish.

The Alard Violin (1715)	
The Duport Violoncello (1711)	Cremonese and Venetian hybrid varnish.
The Betts Violin (1704)	

While engaged in these experiments, I have examined about a dozen of Stradivari's instruments (violins and violas), the varnishes on which were Cremonese and hybrid. I did not observe one pure Venetian (one or two of the varnishes had been tampered with); they were certainly all dichröic, not one of them was coloured.

Not only is there a difference in tint between a Cremonese and Venetian varnish, but there is a most decided difference in the tone which is obtainable by the impregnation of the wood by the two varieties. An instrument treated with a Venetian varnish will possess a tone more resonant, powerful, and brilliant than that obtainable from a precisely similar instrument covered with Cremonese; the derivatives of turpentine of Venice appear to give more resistance to the wood which is saturated with them; the wood of pitch-pine is much more elastic than that of larch.

In contemplating these facts and deductions, it is impossible to avoid reference to the life and work of Stradivari. In the light which has so far been thrown on his career, his aims are sometimes not intelligible; but this novel view gives a possible explanation of facts which other writers have observed and recorded.

Down to the time of Stradivari, if we may judge by the occasional recurrence of brown varnishes, it may be assumed that the Cremonese makers employed some crude or direct method of heating in making their varnishes; if not generally, at least frequently.

All the varnishes of Stradivari which I have seen, or of which I possess illustrations, were, without doubt, made with the water-bath. The first improvement of varnish which Stradivari adopted was therefore the use of the water-bath; if he did not introduce it, he recognized its great advantage, and appears to have invariably availed himself of it.

Up to about the year 1696 we find Stradivari experimenting with the form of his instruments. The " Long Strad." was introduced in 1690; he returned to Amati traditions in 1698 (Hill). What was he seeking ? The softness, equality, purity and volume of tone of the instruments of his predecessors and of his own early life left nothing to be desired. It seems evident that what he sought was greater power and brilliancy. Was not this what he expected to obtain from the " Long Pattern " ? Were not experiments with curves of smaller radii for table and back (such as are to be observed in Stainer's instruments) in the same direction ? Why did he return to Amati traditions (as to form) in 1698 ?

If we may judge from the small amount of evidence before us, he was still using Cremonese varnish in 1696 (*vide* Inlaid Viola). He had exerted his powers in hardening (as far as possible) the Cremonese varnish, and had produced the Tuscan Violin (1690); he could not possibly have gone beyond this varnish in oxidation and dehydration without necessitating an increase of oil, which would obviously defeat his object.

Not long after 1696, the idea of trying the effect of Venetian varnish (*i.e.*, turpentine of Venice) appears to have occurred or to have been suggested to him (the influence of Montagnana appears possible, but there are no means of obtaining any light on this point; so little is recorded of the " great Venetian " that whether he was of Venetian origin or was a Cremonese who migrated to Venice, there is no evidence to show). Then he not only obtained different tints of colour; but the use of Venetian varnish, by imparting increased resistance to his diaphragms, gave him the qualities of brilliancy and power which he had so long sought in vain.

His experiments with form and thickness of wood seem from about 1698 to have ceased; during his great period (1700—1725) he appears to have devoted his attention to the effects of different combinations of Cremonese and Venetian varnishes—of hybridisation. Even so late as 1725 we find him using a pure Venetian varnish—

if the surmise as to the Madrid violoncello described by M. de Try is well founded.

It must be evident that this change of varnish may account for the preference that is given, for large rooms, to the instruments of the pupils of Stradivari and such of his contemporaries as may have acquired the necessary information,—to those of the makers that constitute the Stradivari group or school. The improvement in tone cannot be traced to any considerable change in form or wood. The form of the instruments of Joseph Guarnerius del Jesu, for instance, differs considerably from that of the Stradivari instruments; but we find a similar brilliancy of tone. Copies of the Guarnerius instruments covered with Maggini or Amati varnish lack this brilliancy of tone, as far as my experiments with such violins go.

The remarks of Mr. Hart are most significant in this connection. Observe what he says about the colours:—" The Cremonese is of " various shades, the early instruments of the school being chiefly " amber-coloured, afterwards deepening into a light red of charming " appearance, later still into a rich brown of the Brescian type, " though more transparent." . . . " The Venetian is also of various " shades, chiefly light red, and exceedingly transparent." He had previously made this remark:—" Upon turning to the " Cremonese, we find that Joseph Guarnerius, Stradiuarius, " Carlo Bergonzi, and a few others, used varnish having the same " characteristics, but again different in shade." It is remarkable that he uses precisely the same expression, " light red," to describe the Cremonese at a particular period as he does for the Venetian; then he puts the " light red " into its proper position between amber-coloured and the recurrence of brown; finally he distinctly discriminates the varnish of the Stradivari group. It has already been suggested that Stradivari used the old amber-coloured varnish as lately as 1696 (Inlaid Viola), and that soon after that date he began to use Venetian; it will be presently shown that after 1725 his varnish became more brown, and that his pupils began to push dehydration, the consequent production of brown colour, too far.

To judge by my brief experience, instruments treated with pure Venetian varnish are most brilliant, resonant and powerful, but the tone is not very easy of prefect production; for amateurs, perhaps, not very agreeable to produce. On the other hand, instruments covered with the Cremonese type give out their tone with a facility and a freedom which are delightful to most amateurs. The artiste prefers to feel that resistance to his bow which the Venetian varnish imparts; with a little experience, even the advanced amateur soon lays aside the more facile instrument. Stradivari appears to have sought a *via media;* he must have numbered more amateurs than professionals among his clients.

The evidence given by the small number of instruments in question is capable of the interpretation that Stradivari began the use of turpentine of Venice tentatively, at first mixing it with pine-turpentine so as to produce hybrid varnish, and that he did not try the effect of pure Venetian varnish until after 1720; this would be consistent with the general trend of evolution of the varnishes of Cremona towards increased hardness and solidity.

Some writers have attributed the increased resonance of the instruments of Stradivari's great period to the quality of the wood of construction. Without a long experience, it is impossible to give a decisive opinion; but I am strongly disposed to attribute the superior qualities of his instruments (1700—1725) mainly to the varnish which he then used.

I varnished two violoncellos (by different makers), one with a pure Cremonese, the other with a pure Venetian varnish; the models of the two instruments are practically identical, the wood of the latter is perhaps a little thicker than that of the former. I have played on one or other of them daily for more than a year; my opinion remains precisely what it was on the first trial. The difference in tone can be easily distinguished; the player feels the difference in resistance to the bow. The resonances of the Venetian instrument are incomparably superior to those of the Cremonese; it is also far more brilliant and powerful; the bass strings are particularly fine. It seems to me inconceivable that the striking difference in tone can with justice be attributed to the wood; certainly the superiority of the one instrument does not arise from any want of care or skill in the cabinet-work of the other. From violinists, moreover, I have found that, in their opinion, violins, identical in every respect, have varying characteristics of tone imparted to them by Cremonese and Venetian varnishes.

* * * * * *

Having traced the progress of evolution towards its zenith of perfection, as exhibited in the finest of the warm-toned (colour) instruments of Stradivari, it will now be necessary to trace the evolution of decline.

When the old Italian varnishes came into existence, the exigencies of life under the genial climate of Italy were such that it was of little moment that an instrument-maker was obliged to wait for many months before he could realize, in a current form, the results of his mental and physical labour. It was not until after Antonio Stradivari had passed his prime that change in this respect began to be felt. This admirable workman could afford (as some of his biographers suppose) to spend twenty years of the best part of his life in study and experiment without feeling any stress of pecuniary embarrassment or want, for himself and his family, of the simple requirements of existence. In spite of the tardy realization of his incessant activity—of the small price which he obtained for his masterpieces—he was passing rich—" rich as Stradivari."

But times change. Conditions towards the middle of the eighteenth century were widely different from the good old times; artists and artificers could no longer afford to wait for many months before exchanging work for current coin. A very slow-drying varnish must have been a serious obstacle to men of small capital, living from hand to mouth; this consideration must have driven the violin-makers to seek some means of expediting the varnishing operation. The deeper-coloured instruments were the first result; for not only are the red and red-brown varnishes a little harder than those which are yellow and orange, but they are also more viscous. The dichröic effects become apparent only when the pellicle has reached a certain thickness; with a pale, limpid varnish ten coats will be required to be effective, whereas with a dark thick one an equally good result may be reached with six; this represents not only a saving of labour, but a considerable saving of time, since a week for drying must be allowed between each coat. Then, again, heating over a water-bath for six or eight hours is a small matter with gas at disposal; with a charcoal stove it is a different matter.

My taste and opinion on the question of medium *versus* dark-coloured varnish, agree with those of M. Antoine Vidal; the dark varnish is the beginning of decline (" c'est le commencement de la décadence ").

There are many excuses, if not reasons, for the movement in a downward direction which Stradivari himself commenced, in the later years of his life, and which some of his pupils soon began to push too far. Deep red-brown varnishes were produced which required a larger proportion of linseed-oil for solution, even then were very viscous. With time, it appears that some of these varnishes have fissured or crackelled, while those of Stradivari remain perfect.

The final evolution of decline is seen in the varnishes of Naples (again a purely arbitrary designation). As everyone who knows anything of varnish manufacture must be well aware, the preparation of the siccative oil is a tedious and troublesome process. If the transformation of raw oil is performed by the aid of metallic oxides, it requires a long time before the boiled oil frees itself, by subsidence, entirely from the residue of the oxidant; it is a matter of months of patient waiting. The Neapolitan type appears to owe its origin to this inconvenience.

From my point of view, the Neapolitan varnishes were perfectly natural and legitimate developments from those of Cremona and Venice, although practical difficulties arose which could not, in those early times, have been foreseen.

It occurred to someone that the process of converting raw linseed-oil to the siccative form was a similar one to that employed for producing resins from the turpentines; therefore, why not combine the two operations and thus save time and trouble ?

Colophony was dissolved in raw linseed-oil, or Venetian or other turpentine was mixed with it; this solution or mixture was subjected to the same oxidation and dehydration processes as the turpentines.

As long as oxidation and dehydration are confined within certain limits, the results are perfectly satisfactory: yellow or orange varnishes prepared in this way are transparent, of good colour, and of excellent quality. But when linseed-oil and turpentine are treated together, and the two processes of degradation are carried further, the changes in both do not proceed *pari passu*. Moreover, the oil was originally introduced into the varnish for the purpose of adding to its cohesive quality; if the oil be degraded beyond a certain point, it also becomes a resin—the attribute which was of so great value to the varnish is lost.

In making the Neapolitan varnishes, therefore, it was necessary to bear in mind that the linseed-oil played a dual part: oxidized up to a certain point, it maintained its valuable properties as a siccative oil, the yellow colour which it acquired added a little more of this colour to that of the resin which made up the complement of the pellicle; oxidized and dehydrated beyond this point, the oil became resinous and viscid, excellent for aiding the production of varnishes of very showy red shades, but no longer serving its original purpose.

In careful hands, under the guidance of an informed mind, the Neapolitan varnishes give satisfactory results; but if these varnishes are made without care or knowledge of the principles involved, they lack the true properties of an oil-varnish.

Linseed-oil, by considerable degradation, tends to become a substantive red colouring matter, which veils (more or less destroys) the refractive effects of the resin. Consequently, except in yellow varnishes, the Neapolitan varieties cannot compare in beauty with those of Cremona and Venice. The difference is especially apparent on the tables of instruments, the delicate grain of which is often obliterated almost entirely.

*   *   *   *   *   *

The origin, gradual improvement, zenith of perfection, eventual decline of the old varnishes have now been traced; their evolution, deduced as fairly as possible from existing records, has been compared with that of similar varnishes in my hands. It must surely be admitted that if the varnishes, ancient and modern, are not the same, I have been misled by a most extraordinary chain of coincidences.

There are yet other idiosyncrasies to be observed in both varnishes which are easy of explanation on the assumption that they are identical, but otherwise difficult to understand. It will be noticed, in the descriptions of the old varnishes, that, when they are pale or yellow, they are generally described as lightly and evenly laid on; while the darker varnishes are frequently represented as abundantly used, often clotted and crusted: their application is supposed to have been wanting in care, neatness or skill. I can affirm, from my own observation, that this criticism (as to the fact) is just. The explanation is simple:—The pale varnishes are oxides of turpentine, little dehydrated, very soluble in oil of turpentine, limpid, easy of even application; the pellicles are, or appear to be, comparatively thin. The darker and brown varnishes contain resins much dehydrated, little soluble in oil of turpentine; their viscosity, much greater than that of pale varnish, cannot be decreased without a large increase of oil. The old masters preferred to limit the oil and to do their best with a thick, viscous varnish: the results are in evidence.

Let the critic who is now disposed to cast stones at the old artisans come to me; I will prepare for him a fine, viscous, absolutely clear varnish, of either type, which, if he essays to lay it on an instrument with perfection of technique, will probably conduce to a more charitable frame of mind. My own charity has become unbounded.

*   *   *   *   *   *

There is a consensus of opinion that the old varnishes were of a soft quality; the instruments in existence appear to afford conclusive evidence of this fact, which two centuries have not obliterated or concealed.

All the ancient instruments have the varnish more or less removed from parts of the surface of the back. This removal of varnish has evidently arisen from two principal causes—firstly, the contact of the lining of the cases in which they have been preserved or conveyed; secondly, the friction of the hands and clothing of the players. The " Inlaid Viola " and the " Tuscan Violin " exhibit mainly the effects of the one cause; the majority of instruments have suffered from both.

Many people prefer an instrument from which parts of the varnish have been so removed—it is supposed to add to the general picturesque effect. This is a matter of taste about which it is proverbially useless to argue.

If one of my instruments (which has been varnished for two or three years, carefully finished and polished so that the surface of the back is smooth and even as that of a mirror) be placed in a closely-fitting case lined with silk plush, it may lie for a week or a fortnight without any apparent change. After that time (the higher the temperature the sooner) a dull spot will gradually appear at the point of principal contact between the varnish of the back and the lining of the case. A few weeks later, the varnish will be found to have there received the impression of every fibre and inequality of the lining material. Nevertheless—the varnish is perfectly dry and solid—it may be repolished. If scraped with a knife, it may be removed in fine powder, or it may be chipped off in small fragments.

The workman who fits up the instruments when they are well dried often leaves on the varnish—where he has unavoidably exerted pressure for a considerable time—the exact impression of the skin of his thumb or fingers. I have seen on one of the finest violins of Stradivari a similar impression of the skin of a thumb—whether that of the old master or of a more modern workman cannot now be conjectured.

That this impressibility of the varnish is, from some points of view, a serious practical inconvenience cannot be denied; no doubt it slowly decreases, especially if temperature is maintained above 25° C. (77° F.). It must be conceded, however, that it is impossible to find a varnish permanently elastic internally, yet externally capable of resisting continued pressure.

There can be little doubt that this inconvenience was felt when saving of time became an object, and that it was a factor which affected evolution. That Stradivari was well aware of the beneficial effect of warmth and aëration is evident from the construction of the loft in which he hung his instruments (Hill, 9, 12). It may be supposed that the temperature in such a loft in the middle of a summer day would often exceed 32° to 33° C. (90° F.), with a free current of air: conditions well suited to the maturation of varnish.

It will be observed, however, that the instruments were in the shade, that, apparently, two sides only of the loft were open. The notion that the Italians exposed their instruments to the direct rays of the sun is manifestly erroneous; such a course would be fatal to both instrument and varnish. Experts know well enough that instruments exist of which the varnish, while still immature, has been exposed to the heat of a man's body which has been sufficient to cause fissures and cracks; the temperature of the human body never exceeds about 38° C. (100° F.), whereas the direct rays of the sun, in Italy, may be expected often to reach 55° to 60° C. (130° to 140° F.).

It would be interesting to know at what date the idea of keeping instruments of this kind in wooden cases originated. The oldest lining which I have seen is the rough, woollen material known as baize; this material must have affected the soft varnish in contact with it in a comparatively short time. The modern linings of smooth cloth or of silk plush are undoubtedly a great improvement.

While the modern well-made and sumptuously lined cases are admirably adapted for the conveyance of instruments, and while, as has been shown, they do not suffer in any way from being placed in them for a few days, it is open to question whether these cases are suited to serve as permanent resting places for valuable instruments. Not a few fine specimens have received (to my knowledge and regret are still receiving) irretrievable damage from the damp and mildew which such close cases are liable to engender, if instruments are not used for some years.

The scroll of instruments appears to have been designed with a view to afford facility for hanging. Formerly it seems to have been customary to hang them by the scroll in a suitable cabinet or cupboard, or in an apartment, air having free access to every part of them. I have found it convenient to revert to this ancient usage.

The introduction of the chin-rest now prevents the friction of the chin or beard of the player; it may also be observed that careful persons take means to prevent clothing or hard substances (such as buttons) from damaging their instruments.

The problem of improvement in the permanent resting places of our valued instruments is worthy of further consideration, in the direction that has been indicated.

*   *   *   *   *   *

The conditions attending the preparation of the varnishes of Cremona and Venice, as well as the inconvenience caused by the length of time required for their solidification, may reasonably be considered sufficient to account for a gradual modification of their constitution, but quite insufficient to justify their total extinction in about the middle of the eighteenth century, especially as their loss practically put an end to the violin-making industry which had existed in Cremona for so long a time.

But if it is supposed that nitric acid was in fact the oxidant employed (there are many considerations which support that hypothesis), then a possible explanation can be given.

It is impossible to avoid the suspicion that, from first to last, the Church of Rome not only patronised, but assisted and advised the violin-makers by the intervention of members of her monastic institutions, as she did the architects, painters, and sculptors of the period. Gasparo came from Salo, which appears to have been, although a small town, a seat of ecclesiastical learning where music was cultivated. There is a story recorded that Maggini when in dire necessity was succoured by two monks. It was natural and justifiable that the ecclesiastics should patronise and encourage, by all means in their power, the arts which assisted in the embellishment of their buildings and of their religious services.

It is less easy to understand or to defend the interest which they took in the perfecting and promotion of discoveries and inventions which more properly belong to " the world, the flesh and the devil."

It is asserted that an explosive compound which contained nitre was known to the Chinese even before the Christian era. In India, some such explosive was certainly known long before gunpowder was introduced into Europe.

The explosive which Friar Bacon discovered independently, or of which he obtained information from his missionary brethren in 1216, was little suited to firearms; it was not until the year 1320, when Bartholdus Schwartz introduced the process of granulation, that the history of modern firearms may be said to have begun.

The principal, most costly, ingredient of gunpowder is the nitre, a substance which was far from abundant in the sixteenth, seventeenth, and eighteenth centuries. The natural stores of nitrate in India, China, South America, &c., to which we are now so much indebted, were not then available. Its main source of supply was artificial; beds of decaying nitrogenous organic matter were made under such conditions that the nitrogen was slowly oxidized in the presence of available alkali. Every two or three years, potassic nitrate was obtained from these beds by lixiviation, mixture with wood ashes, subsequent purification by crystallization.

In the manufacture of gunpowder, the almost perfect purity of the nitre is a matter of the first importance; its purification from other salts is not particularly easy. This subject must have required a good deal of patient study. The improvement of gunpowder must have entailed the attainment of very considerable knowledge of potassic nitrate and its reactions with other chemicals, such as sulphur (another of the constituents of gunpowder).

Cremona formerly belonged to the Duchy of Milan. The last of the Sforza, Dukes of Milan, died in 1535. The Duchy then passed under the rule of Spain, and appears to have enjoyed comparative peace until the beginning of the eighteenth century (fighting in a small way, pestilence and famine were ordinary occurrences). The great War of the Spanish Succession then began, involving several of the European Powers in a long and sanguinary struggle. Cremona itself did not escape the horrors of war. By the treaty of Utrecht in 1711 and 1713 the Duchy of Milan was ceded to Austria. Shortly before the middle of the eighteenth century another great European War broke out—that of the Austrian Succession.

The demand for nitre in Europe must have largely increased during the wars of the eighteenth century. The efforts made by

Governments to assure a supply of nitre for the manufacture of explosives were such as can hardly be conceived possible at the present time. It was no unusual thing for a European State to enact that the peasant-farmers should pay a defined proportion of their taxes in saltpetre or nitre, which they were obliged to obtain by the artificial process already described; such enactments have remained in force in some countries during my lifetime.

What means were taken by Austria, within her dominions, for the necessary supply of nitre to the Government during the War of Succession cannot now be easily ascertained (her geographical position in relation to the question must not be ignored); it is at least probable that decrees may have been promulgated and enforced without any regard to the influence of such proceedings on commerce or the industrial arts.

Naples and other towns (such as Bologna) which were not under Austrian rule may have been in a totally different position as to the supply of nitre, and consequently of nitric acid.

It is significant that gunpowder appears to have been, up to the middle of the nineteenth century (perhaps later), one of the State monopolies of Austria.

Whether the occurrence of the War of Succession and the sudden extinction of the Cremonese varnish at the same period was a mere coincidence, or whether the one had an influence on the other, must be left to the reader to judge from the brief facts which have been stated; the question may perhaps be considered worthy of further research.

*   *   *   *   *   *

The question as to whether there existed a secret or not, is not material; but it is of interest, because a secret may have had some influence on the sudden extinction of the varnish, and may account, under certain circumstances, for the complete loss of its method of preparation.

M. Mailand and others have asserted, without much reason, that the maintenance of such a secret, for so long a time, would be impossible; the assumption that similar varnish, or varnish formed from the same basis, was in common use or was to be found in commerce, has been shown to be entirely without foundation.

If the process of manufacture were that which I have adopted, there would be no difficulty in keeping the secret; I could easily have kept it to myself if I had been so disposed. If I divulged it to others, why should they make it public if their interest and livelihood depended on the maintenance of secrecy ? The varnish itself, whether in its fluid state or in the pellicle, affords no clue whatever as to its origin. Even the most accomplished chemist of to-day would be unable to discover how it was produced, much less one of the sixteenth, seventeenth, or eighteenth century.

There happens to be an analogous case of a secret manufacture, which has been well preserved in these later days, connected with the manufacture of glass for optical purposes. The extraordinary thing is that this highly technical discovery should have been made by a simple, but doubtless very intelligent, workman, and that men of science are still unable to ascertain the exact detail on which success depends. This discovery was made by P. Guinand (the son of a working carpenter, of Brenets, in Canton Neuchatel, Switzerland), who was born in 1740. The secret was communicated to several persons, but, nevertheless, it has not leaked out. (Cantor Lecture: " Glass for Optical Purposes " by Richard T. Glazebrook, M.A., D.Sc., F.R.S. Lecture I. Journal of the Society of Arts. 17th October, 1902.)

What evidence is there to show that the Italian violin-makers were not members of a " Guild " ? It may have been a secret society; that would be well in accordance with Italian methods. The use of labels from the earliest times is consistent with its existence, so are the relations which appear to have existed between master, pupil or apprentice and journeyman. Trade Guilds were much in vogue at the period. M. Vidal gives an interesting account of several of these Guilds (in other countries), with their rules or statutes. Only approved artificers were admitted to membership; the laws to which they had to submit were strict, sometimes arbitrary. The rules of such a Guild may explain the reason why Antonio Stradivari, for so many years of his life, used the labels of Nicolo Amati. Only members of the Guild were allowed to use such labels; instruments without the label of a member were not permitted to be sold, under severe penalties.

The existence of a Guild secret would enable a reasonable explanation of the extinction of the varnish and process to be given. If the varnish secret were known only to a certain number of persons, who were not initiated until they became " masters " of the guild—*i.e.*, until they had reached full manhood—and if the use of the secret were arrested for a considerable period from the scarcity of an essential ingredient, it is quite conceivable that the process might die out entirely; those who had practised the art would be driven, by necessity, to seek other varnishes, other methods; there would no longer be any reason (or any means) for teaching the rising generation; the cognoscenti would gradually die out, carrying the knowledge of an obsolete process with them to their graves.

M. Alphonse Daudet (" Tartarin de Tarascon "), who ought to be a competent authority, expresses the opinion that people of the North are not qualified to pronounce judgment on evidence emanating from the South; a person having very little acquaintance with the sunny South must not venture therefore to express an opinion on the stories relating to this matter which have been circulated; but he may be allowed to state that he is in the habit of basing his opinions on evidence of a different character.

*　　　*　　　*　　　*　　　*　　　*

Another point requires some consideration. It has been constantly asserted that the varnishes in question were in common use for other purposes at the period when they were employed by the violin-makers. M. Mailand, with easy access to Continental museums and collections of antique furniture and cabinet-work, was perfectly well aware that examples of this kind of workmanship, covered with the varnish, were not in existence; he therefore had to seek some other support for this theory. He admits that the varnishes which the violin-makers used, " whatever they might " be, were excellent for this special application, since the instruments " which they covered with them have reached us after more than " two hundred years in a fine state of preservation, and since " these varnishes have protected them, while leaving them an " entire liberty of vibration " (9, 10). . . . But, " In effect, at

v. 8

"the period in which the Italian masters worked, the fabrication
"of varnishes was still in its infancy; however, these men, who
"knew their art so well, recognized that those which were made in
"their time and which they had appropriated to their use, although
"bad for other purposes (quoique mauvais pour d'autres besoins),
"were precisely those which best suited their instruments" (4).
He thinks that French polish, varnishes made from copal, amber,
and similar substances, because of their greater solidity, were
vastly superior for all other purposes, but not for instruments.

This argument (founded on a fair amount of imagination) has
a hole in it ! If the varnish was common, then, besides violins,
other wooden articles covered with it should and must have reached
us; if other articles so covered have not reached us, then, in order
to support the assumption of opportunity for general use, it must
be clearly shown that the other artificers had other varnish better
suited to their purpose.

Copal- and amber-varnish, French polish, and spirit varnish in
general are beside the question; for it is quite certain that the
cabinet-makers of the sixteenth century did not either prefer or
reject them, for the simple reason that they were not in existence
at that time. M. Mailand proves to his own satisfaction that the
experts of Bonanni's time (1713) could not dissolve either hard
copal or amber; lac he states to have been first introduced into
Europe shortly after the middle of the seventeenth century; it
was probably many years later before it was commonly used in
alcoholic solution. It will be remembered that, according to
M. Vidal, Louis Guersan (a pupil of Jacques Boquay) was the
first French violin-maker to try spirit varnish for his instruments,
some time after 1735. Did the cabinet-makers of the sixteenth
century, in fact, use varnish which was more solid than that of
Cremona ? M. Mailand himself gives information as to the kinds
of varnish commonly known at that time, by quoting from the
publications of Alexis (1550) and Fioravanti (1564). The former
prescribes potable spirit (*eau de vie*) for the solution of benzoin;
the latter, the same menstruum for benzoin, sandarac, and mastic;
this solvent was clearly available only in small quantity, and is
not strong enough for an effective spirit varnish. The ingredients

of the oil-varnishes were mastic, sandarac, pine-resins of different kinds, linseed-oil and turpentine (the three latter were the preponderating constituents). It is certain that, from these, oil-varnish harder than the Cremonese could not be obtained; quite the reverse. A very little study of the prescriptions given by the various authors cited is sufficient to convince anyone that the best varnish capable of production by the directions given would be vastly inferior in every respect to the varnish used by Maggini, the Amati, the Guarnerii and by Antonio Stradivari. The reason why the cabinet-makers did not use this varnish instead of the very inferior ones at their disposal was simply because they were unable to obtain it.

Now as to the main assertion that Cremonese and Venetian varnishes were and are unsuitable for other purposes. *Primâ facie*, it must be evident that the varnish on a violin or violoncello in daily use, which M. Mailand acknowledges as efficient for the preservation of these instruments for two centuries, is solid enough for the protection and fine enough for the embellishment of the cabinet in which the instruments hang, and for other similar articles of furniture which are not exposed to more severe friction and wear than the instruments.

Prior to the introduction of French polish, chairs and tables were probably polished with the simple compound of beeswax, linseed oil and turpentine, which was generally used for that purpose in Europe up to about the beginning of the last century; it is readily admitted that, except for the top of a dining-table and for other articles of furniture similarly exposed to heat, French polish is an excellent substitute for the crude, simple and laborious polish of the olden-time.

The only way to put an end to these assertions, assumptions and theories as to the unsuitability of Cremonese varnishes for purposes other than the covering of instruments, was to make a practical experiment on a sufficiently large scale. A spacious music-room was built of stone; it was ceiled with wood decorated with wooden mouldings in geometric patterns; the walls were lined and panelled with selected wood of different varieties. The choicest copal varnishes that could be obtained, of various shades, were used to cover parts of the dressed wood; other parts were French polished; the remainder (as well as cabinets for instruments, bookcases and shelves for printed music) was covered with Cremonese varnish of my own preparation. The different varnishes can now be seen and examined, side by side, under identical conditions. The result is conclusive that the Cremonese varnishes are perfectly suitable for the purpose; as may be supposed, their decorative effect is unapproachable.

As to hardness, that is a question of extent of degradation, and of the kind of turpentine chosen as raw material; Venice turpentine producing, other conditions being equal, more solid varnish than pine-turpentine. The reason for this difference has yet to be ascertained. As to durability, for interior use the amount of oil used for instruments is sufficient; for exterior use, my short experience and a few experiments lead me to suppose that increase of oil is necessary to enable any varnish to withstand weather and climate. The ingredient which resists these influences being the oil, and not the resin, of whatsoever kind it may be, the condition of the oil (as to extent of degradation) is a factor which must not be ignored.

*   *   *   *   *   *

The imagination contemplates with pleasure generations of artizans, leading simple and industrious lives, patiently seeking to bring to perfection the various instruments of the violin family which were destined to give unalloyed enjoyment to succeeding thousands of men and women. Malignant rumour has indicated the existence of one black sheep among their number; but, happily, the vague stories which have been promulgated are apparently apocryphal, to say the least, they are of extremely doubtful authenticity. Antonio Stradivari, above all, has left behind him a record of a man of eminent ability and intelligence, of steadfast purpose and untiring industry, pursuing a lofty ideal during a long, unostentatious and blameless life.

Suddenly this charming reminiscence is lost in oblivion. In a few years humanity began to realise that they had sustained a loss which appeared irreparable. A struggle began for the possession of the instruments which the old masters had bequeathed to posterity. The old condition of industry and simplicity was changed to one of craft and deception.

M. Vidal gives a vigorous description of the state of things which ensued. The most prominent and grotesque actor in the scene is Luigi Tarisio, an Italian pedlar of low origin, who, apart from cupidity, appears to have had a passion for the acquisition of the old instruments, the best of which he could not bring himself to part with. At his death, in his miserable resorts, he left behind him a hoard of about 250 instruments, many of them perfect masterpieces, which realized an unexpected fortune for his poverty-stricken heirs. In M. Vidal's book will be found a graphic and amusing description of the man and his methods.

The demand caused by the eagerness of artistes and amateurs for specimens by masters of the greatest renown soon led to its supply. Labels were exchanged and forged, instruments were made up of heterogeneous parts. For many years the best workmen of Europe devoted their energies and talents to the task of producing counterfeits of the old masterpieces, sacrificing their artistic individuality to a degrading traffic in order to obtain the necessaries of modern existence. While every charitable mind will seek to find excuses for these proceedings, it is futile to attempt to disguise the fact that the originating cause was that they found themselves able to obtain for copies (including facsimiles of the labels and imitations of the effects of age and wear) a higher price than their own acknowledged work would bring. If they were not actual perpetrators of fraud, they brought the possibilities of it within the reach of ignorant or unscrupulous dealers. The young artist who copies pictures by old masters for the purpose of increasing his own knowledge and skill, signing the copies with his own name, does that which is perfectly legitimate and proper; but an experienced and accomplished artist who makes a constant practice of copying ancient masterpieces, imitating the signatures and the apparent effects of time and accident, does that which may be excused by extenuating circumstances, but cannot be defended by any sophistry.

Under the sinister influences described, there were both violin-makers and dealers that stood firm to settled principles of probity and ingenuousness; but, unfortunately, there is too much reason to suppose that they were occasionally duped by the productions of their more astute and less scrupulous competitors. The confusion and distrust arising from this state of things was bad enough; what it might have been had the concocters of counterfeits been in a position to use the proper kind of varnish can well be imagined; the varnish was the weak part of the illicit productions which betrayed them.

With the vast increase of wealth during the latter half of the nineteenth century, as well as the growing numbers of artistes and amateurs, the value of good examples of the work of the old Italian masters has been steadily enhanced; it is not surprising that traffic in instruments has proved to be a more lucrative employment than the production of genuine modern ones: the violin-maker, as an artist, has practically disappeared.

There are, nevertheless, instruments made to-day which, as far as wood and workmanship are concerned, are admirable in every respect. The restoration to the artistic violin-maker of the varnish which has been so long withheld from him—the increment which was wanting to enable him to attain his ideal of perfection—is a prospect which cannot be contemplated without satisfaction.

If the views which have been expressed (which originated in the researches of M. Félix Savart) as to the causes of the deterioration of the sounding-boards of pianofortes are well founded, it must be evident that the spirit varnish at present used for them is not the most suitable; it may be expected from all the evidence that the substitution of Cremonese or Venetian oil-varnishes for this purpose must result in improvement of tone when these instruments are new, and in the prevention of deterioration as they grow old.

With increasing education and enlightenment, civilized people will more and more perceive that artistic productions which are base in design or in execution do not necessarily become more desirable because they are old. The value of a masterpiece becomes enhanced by age because of its inherent excellence and its rarity; mean productions become neither admirable nor rare with increasing age.

The dogma that instruments of the violin family improve by age has been so persistently promulgated that it has received general credence; my efforts to obtain real evidence in its support have met with an entirely negative result: whatever evidence exists on the question of tone points in the opposite direction.

Experiments on this subject have, in the opinion of M. Vidal, given rise to the most remarkable phenomena in the history of bow instruments. He relates at length what occurred (68, 69, 70, 71). M. François Chanot (" Capitaine ingénieur de deuxième classe dans " la marine française ") brought before the Académie des Beaux-Arts of Paris, in 1817, a violin of a new form which he had invented. The Académie appointed a commission to judge of its quality of tone. The members of this commission were de Gossec, Cherubini, Catel, Lesueur, Ch. de Prony and Berton. M. Alex. Boucher was chosen as the player, and, in order that there should be no bias, he played on a fine violin of Stradivari and on the new violin in an apartment adjoining that wherein the judges were assembled, so that he could be heard without being seen. " The whole " commission, in three consecutive trials, always thought they " heard the Stradivari when M. Boucher was playing on the new " violin, and *vice versâ* when he played on the Stradivari." The question was decided in favour of the violin of M. Chanot, which, although new and made of fresh wood, was able to bear successfully this trying ordeal. The Académie seem to have been so much surprised at this result that they demanded a new trial before their members (in general meeting) on the 26 July, 1817. Boucher repeated his performance with the same result—the Chanot violin was adjudged to be much superior to the Stradivari.

M. Félix Savart obtained an identical verdict, in 1818, for a violin of his invention. The Commission on that occasion consisted of Ch. de Prony, Cherubini, Catel, Berton, Lesueur, and Biot; the player was M. Lefebvre.

Nevertheless the prestige of these two new violins lasted only two or three years.

The conclusions to be drawn from these experiments, which appear to have been conducted under such conditions as to eliminate all prejudice or bias, are either (1) that the judges were deceived and came to a wrong conclusion, which seems scarcely credible; or (2) that the Stradivari had not improved by age, and (3) that the new violins deteriorated in a very few years.

Similar experiments have been made by myself under the same conditions. The result has been to prove that musicians with a cultivated ear cannot distinguish between the tone of a new instrument and that of those which have been in existence for about two centuries.

All the available evidence is in favour of the supposition that violins do not improve with age. My firm conviction is that instruments which are at present mediocre or inferior, either in appearance or tone, so far from becoming better in either respect with use and age, will decidedly deteriorate, even if they exist for a century or more. Whether instruments which are now good in both respects will maintain these qualities for a great number of years must remain an open question.

It would be some satisfaction to know that in the near future an excellent instrument will be within the reach of any one who seriously desires it and has the intelligence to appreciate it, without troubling our minds about its transmission to posterity. The first thing we have to do is to produce instruments equal to the old ones. If we succeed in doing this we may reasonably expect that the modern ones, like the others, will bear the test of time. What has been done once may be done again. To be satisfied with productions which are admittedly inferior to the old ones, flattering ourselves with the hope that the beneficent hand of time will improve them, is to set up for ourselves the pursuit of a myth. This is certainly no Stradivarian method. He would not have bequeathed to us either unsurpassed masterpieces, or the still more valuable example of a life of lofty and steadfast purpose, if he had contented himself with the indulgence of a vague and fantastic chimera. His own works show that his method was based on crucial tests of his own productions, which led to gradual progress towards his ideal of perfection.

General commiseration is felt for the unfortunate artiste who, of necessity, attempts to convey the expression of thought and sentiment to a critical audience through the medium of an indifferent instrument. My deepest sympathy attends him in his hours of study and practice. He must be a genius indeed who, under such adverse conditions, distances his rival who has the inestimable educational advantage arising from the possession of a sympathetic and resonant violin or violoncello. In my humble opinion, a fine instrument is fully as important a factor in education as it is in display.

*   *   *   *   *   *

The processes herein described are the subjects of Letters Patent in Great Britain and Ireland No. 19,626 of 1902; and in the United States of America No. 754,298 of 1904.

BIBLIOGRAPHY

BERTHELOT. Annales de Chimie. Vols. 38, 39, 40.
Paris. 1853, 1854.

DIETERICH, Dr. Karl. Analysis of Resins (trans. by Chas. Salter).
London. 1901.

ENGEL, Carl. Researches into the early history of the Violin family.
London. 1883.

F TIS, F. J. Biographie universelle des musiciens. *Paris.* 1889.

FLEMING, James M. Old violins and their makers. *London.* N.D.

*GALLAY, J. Les luthiers italiens (nouvelle édition du
Parfait Luthier de l'abbé Sibire). *Paris.* 1869.

GROVE, Sir George. Dictionary of music and musicians
(A.D. 1450–1889). *London.* 1900.

*HART, George. The violin, its famous makers and their imitators.
London. 1880.

HAWEIS, Rev. H. R. Old violins. *London.* 1898.

*HELMHOLZ, Hermann L. F. On the sensations of tone
(trans. by Alex. J. Ellis). 2nd edit. *London.* 1885.

*HILL, Messrs. A short account of a violin by Stradivari, dated 1690.
London. 1889.

* do. do. Gio: Paolo Maggini, His life and work. *London.* 1892.

* do. do. Antonio Stradivari, His life and work (1644–1737).
London. 1902.

HIPKINS, A. J. Musical instruments, historic, rare and unique.
Edinburgh. 1888.

*MAILAND, Eugène. Découverte des anciens vernis italiens
(nouvelle édition). *Paris.* 1874.

*NAUDIN, Laurent. Fabrication des vernis. (Gauthier-Villars.)
Paris. 1902.

NAUMANN, Emil. History of music (trans. by F. Praeger).
London. N.D.

OTTO, Jacob A. A treatise on the structure and preservation of the
violin (trans. by John Bishop). *London.* 1875.

RABATÉ, E. L'industrie des résines. (Gauthier-Villars.)
Paris. 1902.

TINGRY, P. F. The painter and varnisher's guide. 2nd edit.
London. 1816.

*VIDAL, Antoine. Les instruments à archet. *Paris.* 1877.

APPENDIX

———◆———

DETAILS OF THE COMPOSITION OF VARNISHES WHICH HAVE BEEN MADE AND USED FOR COVERING MUSICAL INSTRUMENTS AND FOR OTHER PURPOSES

———————

Colophony and turpentine of Venice are measured by weight (grammes).
Nitric acid, linseed-oil, oil of turpentine by volume (cubic centimetres).
Turpentine of Venice is estimated at 80 per cent. as resin.
Oil of turpentine is estimated at 50 per cent. as resin.

———————

CREMONESE VARNISH

No. 1

Made 13 February, 1901 (*dry way*)

	Parts.	Per cent.
Colophony	100	28·57
Nitric acid 20		
(oxidation reaction)		
Linseed-oil (boiled)	50	14·29
(heated over sand-bath to 120° C.)		
Oil of turpentine	200—240	57·14
	350	100·00

———————

No. 2

Made 19 February, 1901 (*wet way, sand-bath, but not above* 100° C.)

	Parts.	Per cent.
Colophony	100	28·17
Oil of turpentine ... ... 50=	25	7·05
Nitric acid 20		
(oxidation reaction)		
Linseed-oil (boiled)	50	14·08
Oil of turpentine	180—240	50·70
	355	100·00

CREMONESE VARNISH
No. 3
Made 17 *March*, 1901 (*water-bath and water-oven*)

						Parts.	Per cent.
Colophony	...	...	...	...	...	100	23·81
Oil of turpentine	...	...	...	...	60=	30	7·14
Nitric acid	...	...	...	...	20		
(oxidation reaction)							
Linseed-oil (boiled)	...	...	...	...	...	50	11·91
(heated in water-oven (100° C.) for 5 hours)							
Oil of turpentine	...	...	...	...	...	240	57·14
						420	100·00

No. 4
Made 19 *April*, 1901 (*sand-bath*)

						Parts.	Per cent.
Colophony	...	...	...	...	...	100	27·78
Oil of turpentine	...	...	...	...	60=	30	8·33
Nitric acid	...	...	...	...	20		
(oxidation reaction)							
Linseed-oil (boiled)	...	...	...	...	...	50	13·89
(maintained at a temperature of 125—130° C. for about 15 minutes)							
Oil of turpentine	...	...	...	...	...	180	50·00
						360	100·00

No. 5
Made 27 *April*, 1901 (*water-bath and water-oven*)

						Parts.	Per cent.
Colophony	...	...	...	...	...	100	27·78
Oil of turpentine	...	...	...	...	60=	30	8·33
Nitric acid	...	...	...	...	30˙		
(oxidation reaction)							
Linseed-oil (boiled)	...	...	...	...	...	50	13·89
(heated in water-oven about 6 hours)							
Oil of turpentine	...	...	...	...	...	180	50·00
						360	100·00

CREMONESE VARNISH
No. 6
Made 4 September, 1901 (*water-bath and water-oven*)

	Parts.	Per cent.
Colophony	100	25·64
Oil of turpentine	60= 30	7·69
Nitric acid ... ... (oxidation reaction)	50	
Linseed-oil (boiled) ... ... (heated in water-oven 6 to 7 hours)	50	12·82
Oil of turpentine	210	53·85
	390	100·00

No. 7
Made 9 December, 1901 (*water-bath and water-oven*)

	Parts.	Per cent.
Colophony	100	25·97
Oil of turpentine	70= 35	9·09
Nitric acid ... ... (nitrification extended over 4 days) (oxidation reaction)	33·3	
Linseed-oil (boiled) ... ... (heated in water-oven about 1 hour)	50	12·99
Oil of turpentine	200	51·95
	385	100·00

No. 8
Made 9 December, 1901 (*second time*)

	Parts.	Per cent.
Colophony	100	28·17
Oil of turpentine ˉ	70= 35	9·86
Nitric acid ... ... 33·3 (nitrification extended over 4 days) (oxidation reaction)	33·3	
Linseed-oil (boiled)	60	16·90
(heated in water-oven about 6 hours)		
Oil of turpentine	160	45·07
	355	100·00

VENETIAN VARNISH

No. 9

Made 21 February, 1901 (water-bath)

					Parts.	Per cent.
Venice turpentine					100= 80	26·67
Nitric acid ... ... (oxidation reaction)					20	
Linseed-oil (boiled) ... ... (heated over water-bath 1 hour)					40	13·33
Oil of turpentine					180	60·00
					300	100·00

No. 10

Made 24 May, 1901 (water-bath and water-oven)

					Parts.	Per cent.
Venice turpentine					100= 80	30·30
Nitric acid ... ... (oxidation reaction)					24	
Linseed-oil (boiled) ... ... (heated in water-oven about 6 hours)					40	15·15
Oil of turpentine					144	54·55
					264	100·00

No. 11

Made 4 September, 1901 (water-bath and water-oven)

					Parts.	Per cent.
Venice turpentine					100= 80	31·58
Nitric acid ... ... (oxidation reaction)					33·3	
Linseed-oil (boiled) ... ... (heated in water-oven 6 to 7 hours)					33.3	13·15
Oil of turpentine					140	55·27
					253·3	100·00

VENETIAN VARNISH (HYBRID)

No. 12

Made 29 November, 1901 (water-bath and water-oven)

	Parts.	Per cent.
Venice turpentine	100= 80	27·40
Oil of turpentine	16= 8	2·74
Nitric acid ... ... (nitrification extended over 4 days) (oxidation reaction)	32	
Linseed-oil (boiled) ... ... (heated in water-oven about 5 hours)	44	15·06
Oil of turpentine	160	54·80
	292	100·00

No. 13

Made 25 April, 1902 (water-bath and water-oven)

	Parts.	Per cent.
Venice turpentine	100= 80	24·84
Oil of turpentine	100= 50	15·53
Nitric acid ... ... (nitrification extended over 3 weeks) (oxidation reaction)	64	
Linseed-oil (boiled) ... ... (heated in water-oven about 5 hours)	48	14·91
Oil of turpentine	144	44·72
	322	100·00

NEAPOLITAN VARNISH
No. 14
Made 20 March, 1901 (water-bath)

	Parts.	Per cent.
Colophony	100	28·17
Linseed-oil (raw)	25	7·04
Nitric acid ... ·... ... ... 20 (oxidation reaction)		
Linseed-oil (boiled) ... ... (heated over water-bath about 3½ hours)	50	14·09
Oil of turpentine	180	50·70
	355	100·00

No. 15
Made 8 April, 1901 (sand-bath)

	Parts.	Per cent.
Colophony	100	29·20
Linseed-oil (raw)	62·5	18·25
Nitric acid ... ... 12·5 (oxidation reaction) (heated over sand-bath until of a deep brown colour)		
Oil of turpentine	180	52·55
	342·5	100·00

No. 16
Made 30 August, 1901 (water-bath and water-oven)

	Parts.	Per cent.
Venice turpentine ... ... 100=	80	14·50
Colophony	80	14·50
Linseed-oil (raw)	16	2·90
Oil of turpentine ... ... 48=	24	4·35
Nitric acid ... ... 48 (oxidation reaction) (heated in water-oven about 6 hours)		
Linseed-oil (boiled)	64	11·60
Oil of turpentine	288	52·15
	552	100·00